WESTERN
MEMORABILIA

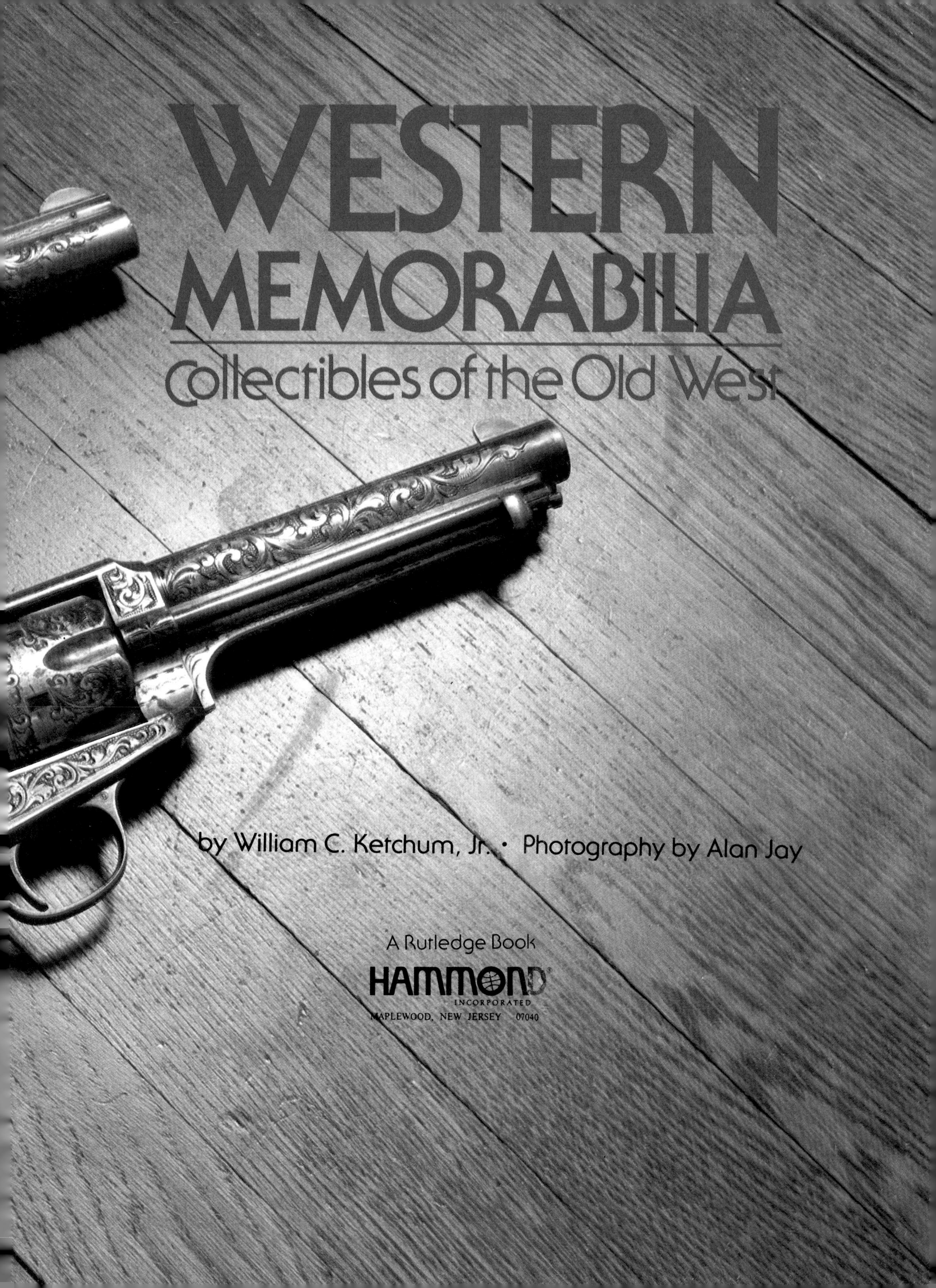

WESTERN MEMORABILIA

Collectibles of the Old West

by William C. Ketchum, Jr. · Photography by Alan Jay

A Rutledge Book

HAMMOND
INCORPORATED
MAPLEWOOD, NEW JERSEY   07040

For Debbie, Jay, and Lori
in lieu of the gold watches
they so richly deserve.

Prepared and produced by Rutledge Books, Inc.
25 West 43rd Street
New York, New York 10036

Published and distributed by Hammond, Inc.
515 Valley Street
Maplewood, New Jersey 07040

First edition 1980

Printed in the United States of America

ISBN 0-8437-3357-8

Library of Congress Cataloging in Publication Data
Ketchum, William C   1931-
    Western memorabilia.

    Bibliography
    Includes index.
    1. The West—Collectibles—Catalogs.   2.   Antiques
—The West—Catalogs.   I.   Title.
NK823.K47   745.1'0978'075   80-15926

Pages 2–3: *Left:* Model 1890 .44-.40-caliber sixgun with gold and silver plating and pearl handle; by Remington; $13,000–15,000. *Right:* Double-action .40-caliber sixgun with gold plate and pearl handle; by Smith & Wesson; $5,000–6,000. Presentation models are one-of-a-kind varieties.
Pages 6–7: Black-and-white photo of cowhands at dinner; Oklahoma panhandle; 1890–95.

Contents

Introduction 6

1. The Original Americans 9

2. The Spanish Colonists 59

3. Mountain Men and Buffalo Runners 83

4. The Cowboys 95

5. Days of Forty-nine 139

6. The Iron Road 165

7. They Plowed the Plains 211

8. Where Roads and Rivers Met 227

9. The Eskimos 245

Acknowledgments 253

Bibliography 253

Index 254

Introduction

Horace Greeley's admonition to "Go West, young man" has never been more applicable than it is today, and in no area is the advice more timely than in that of antiques and collectibles. Collectors are discovering that the western United States—so vast geographically, so diverse politically, economically, and socially—provides a veritable treasure trove of Americana.

Nowhere else are there such rich and varied fields for exploration: Indian artifacts; Spanish-American folk art and furnishings; mining, railroad, and cowboy memorabilia. The West provides all these and many more. Surprisingly enough, it has taken a long time for most people to appreciate this wealth of beauty and history. Some things, such as Indian and cowboy memorabilia, have been collected for many years, but most other areas have been ignored except by local enthusiasts. As late as 1974, the Whitney Museum's landmark exhibition, The Flowering of American Folk Art, contained no examples that could be said to be truly western in origin.

All this is rapidly changing, and interest in western memorabilia is increasing. Painting and sculpture by the great western artists such as Russell and Remington are already prohibitively expensive. Prices for good-quality Indian materials are skyrocketing, and the better ex-amples of Eskimo and New Mexican art are vanishing from the market. The race is to the swiftest and the richest!

Where does this leave the average collector for whom this book is intended? The enormous quantity of western relics insures something for everyone, young or old, rich or poor. The long-forgotten ghost towns and dumps of the mining areas still yield bottles to the digger. Railroad material in the form of iron spikes and glass telegraph insulators can be picked up along the old rights-of-way, and choicer items, such as lanterns, railway china, and advertising materials, are frequently available at reasonable prices. The boom in gold and silver has brought a renewed interest in the "men of '49" and the legion of prospectors that swarmed to the western hills looking for "color." Their artifacts, from picks and pans to large pneumatic hard-rock drills, can still be found in antique shops and secondhand stores or sometimes right where they were dropped in some old mine or mill. But the collector had best get there fast, for some of these items are going back into service in the *new* gold rush of the 1980s!

There's a lot out there for the collector, particularly if he or she is knowledgeable and persistent, but there are some surprises, too. One of these is price escalation; a

second is reproductions and outright fakes. As mountain and prairie memorabilia become more valuable, the temptation to make a fast buck becomes greater. What appear to be Zuni-made kachina "dolls" turn out to have been produced in Taiwan. Woven fabrics from Mexico show up among authentic Navajo blankets and rugs. New Indian (or non-Indian) silver is represented as old, and Colt Peacemakers that never saw service west of Philadelphia suddenly acquire a history of use by Billy the Kid or Bat Masterson. There is nothing more disheartening to the collector than the realization that he or she has been "stung." One of the goals of this book is to provide information that will help people avoid such occurrences, but in the final analysis it is personal knowledge and dependence on a reliable dealer that will prevent disappointment.

Another thing to keep in mind is that many, if not most, of the objects owned and used by the settlers who populated the West between 1850 and 1915 were not made in the West. They were manufactured east of the Mississippi River. The initial settlement of the Great Plains and the Pacific coast was followed so swiftly by the coming of the transcontinental railroads that the eastern factories were able to supply most pioneers with nearly everything they needed, from furniture to clothing and kids' toys. Eastern manufacturers even crated up a type of wooden prefab house and shipped it west to the treeless prairies!

One result of this was that it was quite a while before local industry could get a foothold, and the collector—like the local museum—is going to find that a lot of things with a strong history of western use have Pittsburgh or Boston labels. Which is perfectly all right; it doesn't make them one bit less western. Any piece used in the Old West, whether it was taken there in a covered wagon or carried out on the Southern Pacific, is a legitimate western collectible. But any time you can find something marked as made in Denver, San Francisco, or some other western town, you will value it all the more.

This book is not only a collector's guide to types and styles in the field of western collectibles—it is also a price guide. For years, enthusiasts of western memorabilia have been faced with the problem that most guides are compiled in the East or Midwest and are focused primarily on antiques and collectibles of those areas. This book focuses on those items found in the western states. As such, we hope that it will prove of assistance to the many thousands of collectors who by their interest and efforts are preserving the great western heritage.

The Original Americans

During the past decade a great many books have been written about the relationship between the western Indians and their white conquerors. Because most of these works portray the Indian as a noble innocent and his foes as ruthless oppressors, they tend to ignore or obscure a great deal of available information about the history and customs of the original Americans.

Though linked in broad groups by linguistic similarities and a common Asiatic origin, Indians varied as much as their foes in culture and disposition. There were sedentary and peaceful farming tribes, such as the corn- and bean-raising Hopi of northern Arizona and the Papago of the Colorado River valley. These groups confined themselves to a specific, limited area that they defended when necessary.

There were also many nomadic and warlike tribes, such as the Blackfeet and the Apache, who ranged back and forth across the Great Plains, following the buffalo herds. Hardy and ferocious, they accepted no boundaries that were not imposed by force, and they were, long before the coming of the white man, in a state of more or less constant war with their neighbors.

The Spanish encountered these rovers in the mid-sixteenth century, and one of their writers described them as follows:

> These Indians live or sustain themselves entirely from the cattle [buffalo], for they neither grow nor harvest maize. With the skins they build their houses . . . clothe and shoe themselves; from the skins they make ropes and also obtain wool. With the sinews they make thread, with which they sew their clothes and also their tents. From the bones they shape awls. The dung they use for firewood. . . . The bladders they use as jugs and drinking containers. They sustain themselves on the meat, eating it slightly roasted and heated over the dung. Some they eat raw; taking it in their teeth, they pull with one hand, and in the other they hold a large flint knife and cut off mouthfuls. They eat raw fat without warming it. They drink the blood just as it comes out of the cattle. . . . They have no other food.
>
> These people have dogs. . . . They load these dogs like beasts of burden and make light pack-saddles, cinching them with leather straps. When the Indians go hunting they load them with provisions. When the Indians move, for they have no permanent residence anywhere, since they follow the cattle to find food, these dogs carry their homes for them. In addition to what they carry on their backs, they carry the poles for the tents, dragging them fastened to their saddles.

There was yet a third group, the subsistence-level food gatherers, such as the so-called digger Indians of California, people who neither farmed nor hunted but who lived solely on the nuts, berries, and even grasshoppers that they scavenged in the barren coastal hills.

These various Indian groups were affected differently and at different times by the coming of the white men. The farmers stood and fought for their lands, but were quickly overrun. By 1690 the Spanish, despite setbacks during the Pueblo Rebellion, had enslaved the Zuni, and the other sedentary tribes of the Southwest soon went the same way.

The diggers, few in number and virtually without a tribal social structure, never presented a real threat to the newcomers and were largely ignored. As the rich valleys of California were settled, first by the Spanish and later by the Anglos, the Indians retired further into their hills, where most eventually perished from white-induced diseases and alcoholism.

The Plains tribes were another matter, and the half-century of intermittent warfare between them and the whites was as bloody and tragic as it was inevitable. Long before 1800 these red men had served notice that they would fight for their lands. Seventeenth-century Spanish colonists in New Mexico and Arizona had come to fear the Apache, who would sweep out of the hills to burn a hacienda and then vanish without a trace; in 1720 Spanish efforts to colonize the central plains were largely abandoned following a crushing defeat inflicted on an expeditionary force sent to the Platte River. The victors that day were the Pawnee, a tribe destined to play a major role in coming hostilities.

Before this conflict could take place, some sort of parity between the opposing forces was required (something that was always lacking in the encounters between the invaders and the farmers and diggers). The great equalizers—the horse and the gun—were provided by the invaders themselves.

Though there had been horses in the Americas during past geological epochs, they were long gone when the first bands of what were to become the American Indians crossed the Bering Sea land bridge into the Northwest. Consequently, when the Spanish reintroduced the horse, it was something new to the Indians. Some thought it was a god, but all recognized its utility. Even before 1600 Indian bands were raiding

Snake Dancer kachina; Hopi; 1900-10; $500-575. There are over three hundred standard kachina figures and another two hundred that are occasionally carved. Wood is the usual construction material, and the better the carving and painting, the more desirable the piece.

Combination war club and quirt; Sioux; ▲ 1870-80; $700-800. This sculptural piece is hand carved and decorated with leather and a feather. It was collected at the time of (and was probably used in) the Great Plains wars of the late 19th century.

the ranchos for horseflesh and capturing and taming horses from the multiplying herds of strays.

A few tribes, chiefly in California, regarded the horse as a food source, but the Plains tribes saw it as something else—a source of rapid transportation across the endless prairies. By the 1690s, the Pawnee were trading for steeds at Santa Fe, and less than a century later the Shoshoni were riding them into combat in the Columbia River basin. Horsemen ranged across the entire width of the western plains.

Utilization of the horse had a profound impact on the life of the western tribes. Some, like the Blackfeet and the Comanche, became superb horsemen, terrifying in warfare. With their new mobility they could control vast areas and destroy or drive out tribes that distance had previously protected.

Moreover, the horse appeared at a moment when more easterly Indians like the Sioux and Crow were being forced westward not only by the pressure of white settlement, but by assaults from neighboring tribes. This constant westward flow was a fact of Indian life during all of the nineteenth century, with many different tribes laying claim in turn to the same geographic area, which makes it difficult to determine, for purposes of compensation or otherwise, true tribal "homelands."

The introduction of the horse also greatly modified how many red men lived and dressed. With increased travel, it became necessary to replace fragile pottery with unbreakable skin and basketry vessels. Elaborate warbonnets and beaded horse trappings became important craft objects, and trading, with whites or other tribes, became a way of life.

The gun was fundamental to Indian defense against the white onslaught. As far back as the eighteenth century, smooth-bore "trade guns" were being obtained from northwestern fur traders and through the various Spanish settlements. Yet the tribal army that exterminated Custer's troops in 1876 could muster but a single rifle for every two warriors.

But the Indians did well with the few guns they had. Though powder and shot (and therefore practice) were always in short supply, many Indians became good shots, particularly from horseback. Riding at a full gallop on his pony and carrying extra rifle balls in his mouth, the brave would load, aim, and discharge his weapon, often from over or even under his horse's neck.

Nor was the rifle used only in warfare. It also provided the tribes with a means of obtaining meat and skins in a quantity sufficient to allow for trade with the fur-hungry whites. Thus, since the Indians needed iron and other trade goods as well as weapons, the two cultures were drawn together by their mutual need for trade, even though that trade was itself a continuing source of friction.

The first easterners to maintain continuous contact with the western natives were the fur traders of the upper Missouri River, and their relationship with the red men mirrored that which was to come throughout the West. At first trading was more or less peaceful, then disputes and the seemingly inevitable clash of cultures led to skirmishes. By 1811 a traveler in the area described elaborate defense preparations as necessary because of "the hostility of the Sioux bands who, of late, have committed several murders and robberies on the whites and manifested such a disposition that it was believed impossible for us to pass through their country."

Relations were unsettled throughout the next decade, culminating in 1823 with the ambush killing of fifteen employees of the Missouri Fur Company by the Arikara. In response to this, six companies of troopers were dispatched from Fort Atkinson to bombard the Arikara villages. The dreaded "bluecoats" had appeared in the West, and for the next seventy years it would be these soldiers who would pursue, fight, and eventually subjugate the Indian warriors.

The fur trappers and traders, like their unwilling hosts, were transients and, as such, they might have been tolerated. But in 1840 the first wagon train navigated the Oregon Trail. From this time on, the fact of permanent white settlement was brought home forcefully to the western tribes.

While this settlement certainly precipitated the Indian Wars, it is not fair to say that the whites stole the Indians' lands. In most cases the tribes had no permanent place of abode; they wandered over the land. Thus when the federal government attempted to buy "Indian lands," its agents encountered an insuperable cultural barrier. The Indians had no concept of ownership as the whites understood it, nor any real form of tribal government. One "chief" (there were many in each tribe) might sell a piece of property, while another and his followers might occupy it the next day—and with as much right.

There is an uglier side of the matter. While Indian agents attempted to buy land (and often had to "buy" it several times from different tribal representatives), this fair dealing was counterbalanced by other official and unofficial acts, particularly the forcing of the tribes off lands previously reserved to them when it was discovered that these lands held valuable mineral or forestry wealth. This activity led directly to some of the most savage tribal uprisings.

It is necessary to say a word about the protagonists in this struggle. The Indian was always a part-time warrior. Raids on other tribes and, later, battles against the whites, were an avocation, something to pursue after the season's buffalo hunt was concluded, with the intention of providing loot and personal glory for the participants. It was always difficult to negotiate permanent peace treaties with the Indians because they had a very different concept of "peace."

As fighters the Indians were an enigma to the whites. They lacked discipline in the western sense, having no central authority or overall strategy. Accordingly, in a pitched battle (Little Big Horn was a notable exception), they usually fared poorly against trained soldiers or even against a well-organized wagon train. The plainsmen excelled in ambush and lightning hit-and-run raids. For this they were called cowards by many who opposed them, but it wasn't cowardice, merely a matter of style and temperament.

Against these irregulars were aligned the "bluecoats," government conscripts on foot and horse who never numbered more than a few thousand in the West. They were paid no more than sixteen dollars a month and were recruited from the ranks of immigrants, hoboes, debtors, and even prisoners. They were so uneducated that officers were at first unwilling to issue them the newly available repeating rifles for fear that they could not operate them! No fear—both the recruits and their foes learned only too well how to manipulate these deadly killers.

The battles fought between these protagonists have become the stuff of legends: Sand Creek, the Fetterman Massacre, Beecher Island, Adobe Walls, and, of course, Little Big Horn. Some of these engagements can be dignified by the term "battle," but most were random skirmishes or massacres of white settlements or Indian villages. In each case the fighting was characterized by cruelty and deceit on both sides.

Historians have called many of the regional conflicts "wars": the Bannock War of 1878, the great Sioux War of 1876, and so on. But they were no more wars in the western sense than the individual engagements were battles. Some perspective on this matter may be gained from the fact that between the end of the Civil War and the last clash between regular army forces and Indians at Leech Lake, Minnesota, in 1898, there were some 938 engagements. Yet in all these "battles," federal forces lost only 1,100 men, an average of slightly more than one per skirmish.

These figures can never tell the full story of the Indian Wars. Minor though they may have been on a national or world scale, they left behind a legacy of bitterness between whites and Indians that is yet to be erased.

Moreover the effect on the lives of the western tribes, which numbered perhaps a half-million persons in 1840, can never be underestimated. The craft and culture of these primarily nomadic peoples were based on a relationship to nature that was largely destroyed by the killing of the bison and the imposition of reservation life. It is a tribute to the resiliency of Indian character that the red man has preserved, under the most difficult conditions, a major portion of his language, arts, and folklore. Today, collectors, some of whose ancestors feared and fought the western tribes, are eagerly seeking out their artifacts, both artistic and utilitarian.

Pipe in catlinite inlaid ▶
with pewter with
wooden stem; Northern
Plains; 1860–75;
$250–300. Catlinite, a
red-hued fine-grained
stone, has been
preferred as
pipe-making material
for a long time by the
western tribes.

Pottery bowl; Zuni; 1905–15; $800–1,100. ▲
This bowl is decorated with a polychromed
figure of an Indian warrior on
horseback—such figures are rarely seen on
southwestern ceramics.

Lakone Mana kachina; Hopi; 1890–1900; ▲
$550–650. Although doll-like in appearance,
kachinas are not dolls, but are religious
instructional figures intended to acquaint
children with tribal deities.

Watercolor, *Black Foot Warrior;* by Paul Surber; 1979; $1,500–1,700. Surber is well known for his attention to detail and accurate depictions of 19th-century Indian dress. ▼

Weapons, Clothing, and Accessories

Before the coming of the white man, the clothing, weapons, and household goods of the western Indians were completely natural in origin; they were made by hand from stone, wood, skins, and other material found locally or obtained in trade with other Indians.

The introduction of European trade goods, as early as the seventeenth century, had a profound effect on native life and crafts. The bow and arrow and the spear or lance, the basic warriors' weapons, were replaced wherever possible by the more efficient gun and the wrought-iron trade ax. Imported iron replaced stone for knife blades and arrowheads.

Though clothing continued for the most part to be made from well-tanned elk and deerskin, the materials used in decorating such garments also changed. Porcupine quills used in embellishing everything from moccasins to storage boxes were supplemented by tiny glass ''seed beads'' obtained from traders, and natural dyes derived from roots and plants were replaced by factory-made colors.

These material changes are important to the col-

lector because the great majority of available Indian artifacts were made during the period when these new materials were available.

Changes in the substances used in making Indian craft objects usually had little or no effect on the basic techniques of construction employed. Things were still made by hand and still decorated with age-old signs and symbols. Such patterns as the points of the compass, the spiderweb, the sun and the moon, appear over and over on Indian creations. All such decoration has religious significance. As an example, the circle was employed to signify unity, both tribal and universal. The abstract quality of such decoration has long had strong appeal for certain collectors.

Many more collectors can admire American Indian weapons, clothing, and household objects, both for the important part they played in the history of our country and for their manifestation of the virtue of patient craftsmanship, a virtue that can be readily appreciated in today's mass culture in which all too often getting the job done as quickly as possible is the only goal.

Folk art ▶ representation of Indian encampment; 1920–30; $225–275. Possibly designed as an educational exhibit, this work accurately depicts a Plains Indian tepee.

Bronze sculpture, *Red Skin Blue Coat*; signed by Carl Pugliese; dated 1974; $1,200–1,400. Many Indians served as scouts for federal troops fighting in the West. ▼

▲
Bronze sculpture, *Nakoma and Nakomis*; cast in 1974 from a 1924 model by the architect and sculptor Frank Lloyd Wright; $1,800–2,200.

◄
Bronze representations of famous Indian chiefs; signed by Gerson Frank; dated 1978. *Left: Chief of the Sioux;* $2,000–2,200. *Right: Keokuk, Chief of the Sauk and Fox;* $2,200–2,500.

Polychromed bronze sculpture, *Dressed to Kill;* ▲
by Carl Pugliese; 1978; $1,500–1,700. This work
depicts an Indian warrior preparing for the
warpath.

Beaded belts; Plains Indians; 1910–30. *Top:* With ▶
playing-card design; $150–180. Playing cards
were introduced into the Indian culture in the
mid-19th century, and card playing soon
became a popular pastime. *Bottom:* Initialed ES
and probably made for tribal use; $175-225.

Detail of beaded and woven wool horse blanket decorated with brass bells; Plains Indians; 1910–20; $800–950. American Indians are regarded as the world's finest bead workers. Like the beads, the bells were trade items, probably made in Europe and imported for sale to the western tribes. ◄

Moccasins in beaded deerskin; Arikara; 1880–1900; $135–160 the pair. Differences in value for beadwork articles are usually based on quality of the work, rarity, and condition. ▼

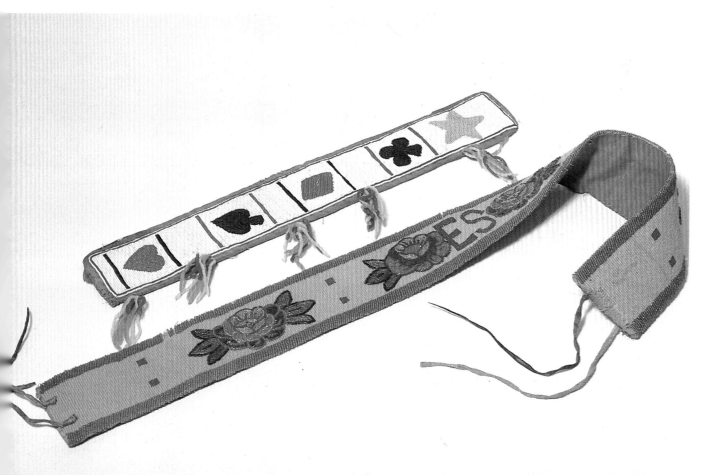

Bronze sculpture of Indian and horse; ▶
signed by Clem Spampinato; dated 1951;
$7,500–8,500. Even an Indian could be
unhorsed by the half-wild prairie pony.

Bronze sculpture, *The American Breed;*
signed by Lucille Hampton; dated 1969;
$3,200–3,500. Indians were skilled
horsemen, and they turned the horse into
a formidable ally in their battles against
the whites. As may be seen here, they
traditionally rode bareback. ▼

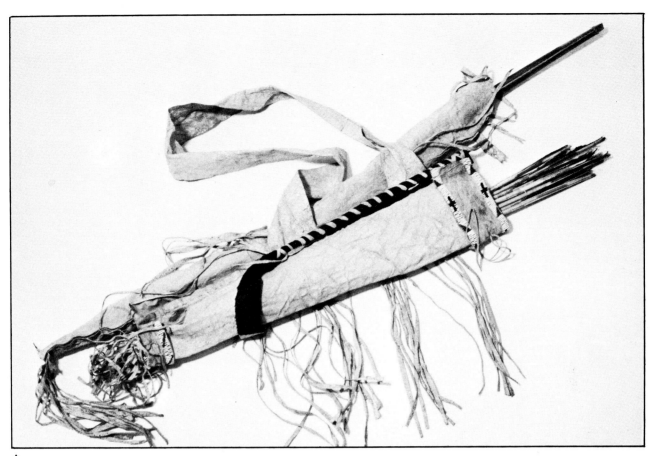

▲
Elk-skin quiver, wooden bow and arrows; Jicarilla Apache; 1915–25; $475–550. The bow and arrow is the traditional long-range weapon of the American Indian and is still in limited use. Sets complete with matching quiver are hard to find today.

Paint-decorated bow and arrows; possibly Blackfoot; 1860–70; $300–400. Note that all but one of the arrows are tipped not with flint but with iron obtained in trade. ▼

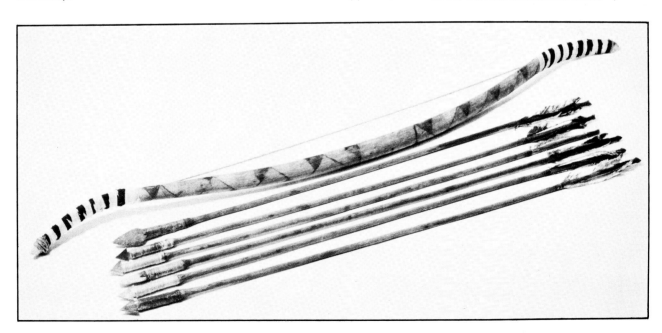

Doll in buckskin with beadwork moccasins, belt, ▶
and cape; Plains Indians; 1900–10; $375–425.
This well-made doll has human hair and painted
eyes and mouth. Early Indian dolls in good
condition are hard to come by.

Blanket in wool; Navajo; 1920–25; $450–525.
Blankets have been an important southwestern
trade item for a long time, and today they are
among the most sought-after Indian collectibles. ▼

Watercolor, *Autumn Skies;* by Paul Surber; ▲
1979; $11,000–12,500. This contemporary
painting depicts a band of Plains Indians
encamped on the western prairie.

Cape; Mandan; 1890–1910; $700–825. This
attractive piece is enhanced by the addition of
cylindrical trade beads and cowrie shells
obtained in trade with West Coast Indians.
Capes with beadwork decoration are relatively rare. ▼

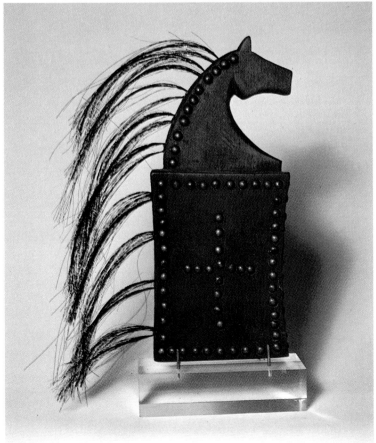

Dance board in wood, horsehair, and leather;
Omaha Sioux; late 19th century; $750–1,000.
These rare and highly decorative pieces were
held in the hand while dancing and had
important religious significance.
◄

23

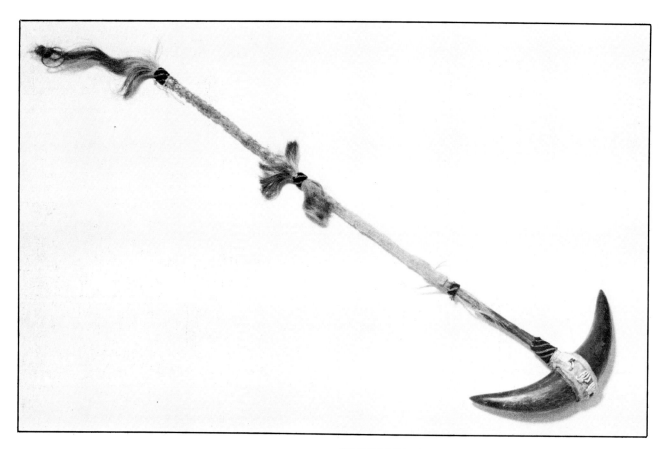

War club made from cow horns and decorated with seed ▲ beads and hair; 1920–25; $175–225. Very lightly made, this piece was probably a tourist item.

▲
Spear thrower in carved stone; Northwest Coast tribes; 19th century; $900–1,100. The Tlingit, Haida, Kwakiutl, and other tribes of the Far Northwest are recognized as among the finest carvers the world has ever seen. Their work brings the highest prices of all Indian artifacts.

◄
Collection of projectile points and blades; both prehistoric and historic; $200–250 the set. Collecting ''arrowheads,'' far from being a child's pastime, is a subtle art involving substantial archeological knowledge.

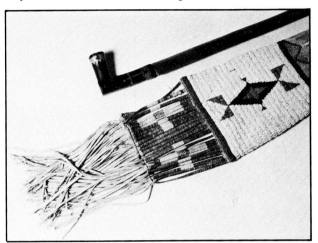

Hudson Bay-style pipe-tomahawk in wrought iron with handle decorated with brass studs and feathers; Northern Plains; 1850–70; $550–750. Trade axes were so superior to the stone product that every brave coveted one.

Top: L-shape pipe in polished black stone inlaid with pewter; Northern Plains; 1860–70; $250–300. *Bottom*: Beaded pipe bag; Sioux; 1890–1900; $650–750. Pipes and the bags in which they were stored were regarded as ceremonial objects and were decorated with great care and skill. ▼

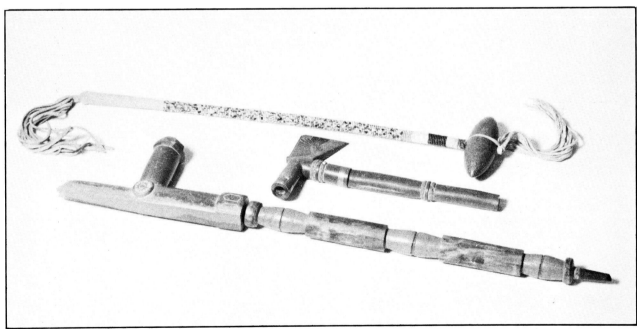

Top: War club in polished stone with seed-bead-decorated ▲ handle; Plains Indians; 1880–1910; $200–275. *Center:* Catlinite or Minnesota red sandstone pipe in form of a pipe-tomahawk banded in pewter with original stem of wood; 1890–1900; $375–450. *Bottom:* Catlinite pipe with embossed decoration and replacement stem; 1880–1900; $250–300.

Oil painting, *The Sergeant;* by Don ▲ Troiani; 1979; $4,800–5,000. Troiani is one of the leading contemporary painters of the American West. The scene depicted is one of the many skirmishes between Indian war parties and the U.S. cavalry.

Polychromed basketry; 1910–30. *Left:* ▶ Pestle-type tray; Columbia River Valley; $175–250. *Center:* Lidless box; Northwest Coast: $450–575. *Right:* Rattle-top basket; Tlingit; Alaska; $900–1,200. Gravel or birdshot in a woven compartment of the basket makes a rattling sound when the basket is shaken. These pieces are rare.

Watercolor, *The Rifleman;* by Don Troiani; 1978; $1,000–1,200. ◄

Ceramic tile with polychrome decoration; Zia; 1940–50; $60–70. Tile is not a traditional Indian pottery form, and this piece was made for sale as a tourist item. ▼

Beadwork; Plains Indians; 1900–30. *Top:* Gauntlets, or wristlets; $70–85. *Center:* Gloves in beaded deerskin; $110–135. *Bottom:* Cuffs; $90–120. Thousands of tiny pieces of glass, known as seed beads, may be used in a single piece of Indian beadwork. ▼

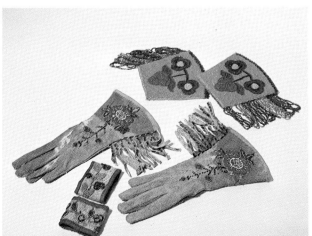

Pipe bag decorated with beadwork; Sioux; 1880–90; $350–425. Decorated with stylized dog figures, this so-called tepee bag is fringed in deerskin. ◄

27

Extremely rare and finely carved stone pipe; Haida or Tlingit;
1860–70; $3,500–4,000. Museum-quality pieces such as this
are seldom available to the average collector. ▼

Drum in lambskin over wood; California; 1930–40; ▲
$100–125. Though probably a tourist item, this piece's value
is enhanced by the primitive painting on its head.

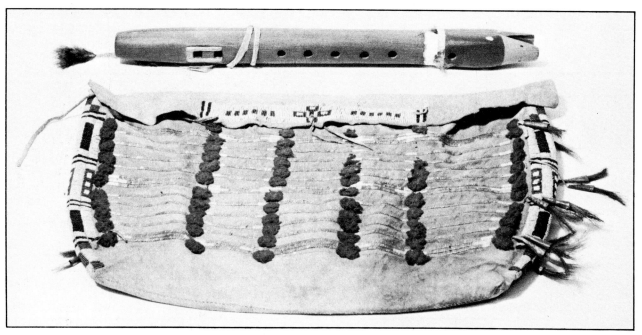

Dance flute in painted wood and carrying pouch in beaded ▲
leather; Mandan or Hidatsa; 1900–15. Flute; $150–200.
Pouch; $350–400. Music had great ceremonial importance
for the Indians.

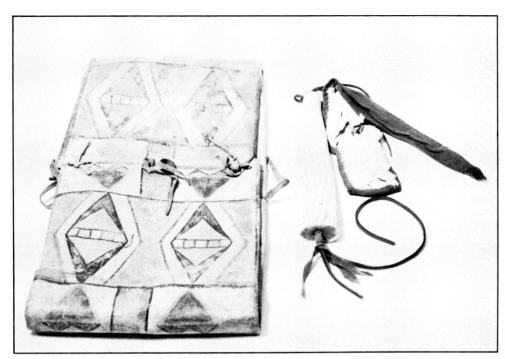

◄
Left: Parfleche, or container, in rawhide; Northern Plains; 1880–1900; $250–325.
Right: Horseman's quirt in elk antler trimmed with leather, cloth, and fur; 1900–15; $75–90.

Man's beaded shirt decorated with ermine and leather fringe; Plains; 1895–1905; $850–1,000. Beaded in red, white, and blue, this shirt is a fine example of Indian craft. ▼

Household accessories; North Dakota, probably Mandan. ▲
Left: Burl bowl; 1870–75; $165–210. *Center left:* Hide scraper with elk-horn handle and steel blade; 1860–80; $85–90. *Center right:* Early trade knife with scabbard in beadwork; 1890–1900; $165–245. *Right:* Dipper in buffalo horn; 1870–80; $60–75.

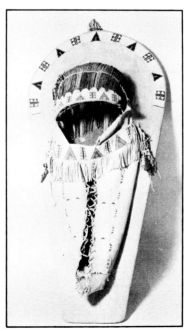

◄
Finely beaded and decorated cradle board in tanned deerskin embellished with seed beads and mounted on a willow frame; Ute; 1920–30; $1,200–1,500. Good-quality cradle boards are quite rare.

Elaborately beaded horse trappings in red, green, white, ▲ and yellow; Plains; 1900–10; $200–275. The value the Plains Indian placed on his horse is reflected in the quality of the beadwork with which he adorned it.

29

Top: Pipe bag in beads and quill work; Sioux; 1880–90; $700–800. Dried and stained, porcupine quills were used by Indians for decoration before the introduction of trade beads and continued in use together with beading. *Bottom:* Pipe bag in beaded deerskin; Plains Indians; 1870–80; $550–625.▼

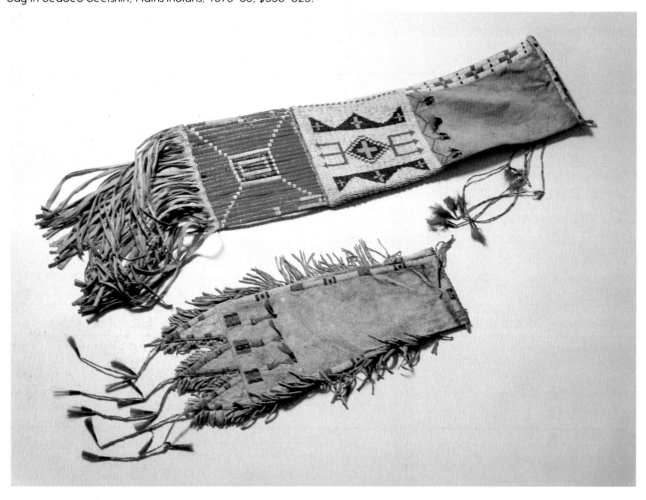

Beaded belt; Plains Indians; 1890–1910; $190–230. This is a
particularly well-done example of a common beadwork form. ▼

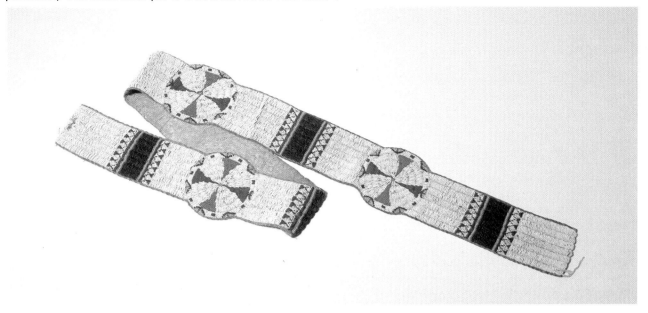

Watercolor of Kiowa medicine man treating patient; by ▲
native American artist David Williams (Tos Que); 1970s;
$600–675. Although many artists have painted the western
tribes, very few are true Indians.

Rugs and Blankets

Since well before 1900 American collectors have been attracted to the weavings produced by the western tribes. The Navajo, the Hopi, and other southwestern Indians have woven blankets for many generations, at first using homegrown cotton, then, after the introduction of sheep by the Spanish, wool.

Earlier textiles were intended primarily for weaving, and ownership of the finest examples, called "chiefs' blankets," was a mark of tribal distinction. These pieces were also traded to nonweaving tribes and were even used as a form of currency.

Part of the blanket's value was the many hours its creation took, but more important was the design, and certain weavers were locally famous for their innovations and adaptations of traditional patterns. Shoulder blankets, striped and banded blankets, a variety of children's coverings, and three distinct types of chiefs' blankets were produced during the period 1850–1900.

These were all woven by men and women using an upright loom of Navajo invention and were colored with natural herb or vegetable dyes. Certain villages and areas became famous for their textiles, and for these villages blanket weaving assumed an important role in the domestic economy.

Like most native crafts, weaving did not escape the effects of western culture. During the early 1870s quality factory-made blankets such as those made by the famed Hudson Bay and Pendleton companies became available in quantity from white traders, and Indians adopted these new coverings with enthusiasm.

It appeared that the weaving tradition might come to an untimely end, but the craft was saved by the first wave of western tourism. Artists, tourists, and military men were drawn to the bold geometric patterns and bright colors of the native weavings and began to buy them in quantity. However, because the whites wanted decorative objects—wall hangings or rugs—rather than wearing apparel, the weavers changed their style. They wove deeper, heavier pieces, changed shapes and designs, and began to employ commercial aniline dyes to speed up production.

The judgment of the native craftspeople and the white merchants who sold their creations proved sound. The textile craft flourished once more, and it has continued to do so. Today there are a dozen localities in the Southwest where Indian rugs and blankets are made, and textiles are among the most popular of western collectibles. Pre-1900 blankets bring hundreds of dollars, and the highly desirable pictorial blankets reach prices well into the thousands. So heated is the market that enthusiasts must constantly be on the lookout for inferior Mexican-made imitations designed to fool the unwary.

Very large rug in brown, ▲
white, and tan wool; Navajo;
1900–10; $750–900.

◄
Rug in red, tan, brown, and
white wool; Navajo;
1900–10; $550–675. This is in
the TicNosPos style, which
features
strongly bordered
multicolored geometric
designs.

◄
Rug in orange, gray, black, and tan wool; Navajo;
1920–25; $675–750. This is in the so-called diamond
pattern in a rather coarse weave.

33

Small square child's blanket in orange, red, gray, and black wool; 1920–30; $250–325. Children's blankets were probably the first wall hangings. ▼

Diamond-pattern rug in red, blue, brown, gray, tan, and ▲ white wool; Navajo; 1890–1900; $900–1,050. The bold geometrics and multiple colors classify this as a so-called eye dazzler.

▲
Serape-style blanket in red, white, gray, tan, and black striped wool; Navajo; 1900–10; $150–200. Intended to be worn, serapes are functional as well as decorative.

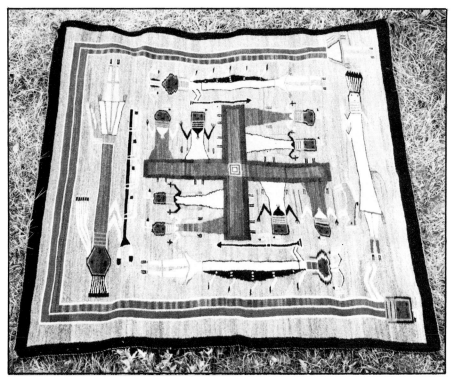

Magnificent Yei-style, or pictorial, rug in blue, white, tan, brown, and black wool; Navajo; 1920–30; $20,000–25,000. This rare, one-of-a-kind piece of weaver's art is peopled with figures adapted from a Navajo sand painting.

Yei-style rug or blanket in red, gray, tan, and brown wool; 1925–35; $7,500–9,000. This valuable piece is peopled with forest animals: the elk, the wolf, and several birds. ▼

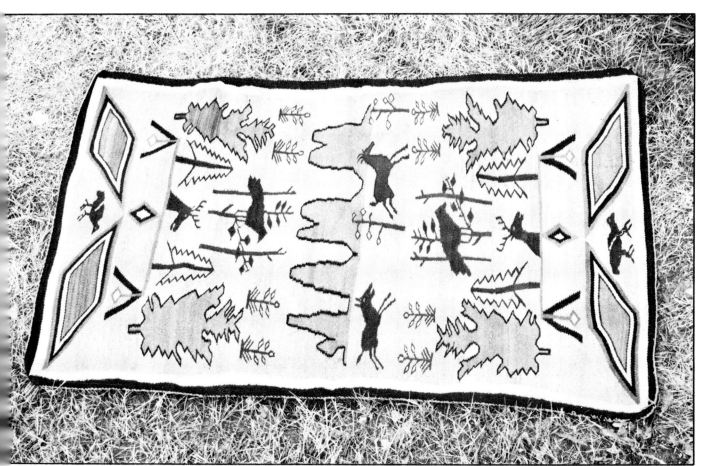

Child's blanket or small throw rug in red and gray wool; Navajo; 1940–50; $130–170. Pieces such as this were made quickly for sale to tourists. ▼

Diamond-pattern blanket in red, black, white, and gray ▲ wool; Navajo; 1920–30; $650–725. Bold patterns and strong borders characterize the best southwestern weaving.

Small child's blanket ▶ or throw rug in orange, black, and gray wool; 1935–45; $200–275.

◄ Geometric-pattern rug featuring terraced design on two sides in red, black, tan, and white wool; Navajo; 1920–30; $750–825. As is the usual case, white areas are of undyed natural wool.

Modified diamond-pattern rug in red, brown, black, and ▲ white wool; Navajo; 1925–35; $600–700. Like most post-1900 pieces, this rug is colored with commercial aniline dyes.

Kachinas

The Pueblo peoples such as the Zuni and the Hopi have, despite the inroads of white civilization, maintained the most stable and traditional of all Indian societies. This is the result, in large part, of their religious system, in which the doll-like kachina figures play an important part.

Unlike most western Indians, the Pueblos established settled agrarian communities at a very early date. One of these settlements, Oraibi, has been continuously occupied for over a thousand years. Dependent upon their crops for a living, the Zuni and Hopi coordinated their social, governmental, and religious systems to the cycle of the seasons.

Elaborate ceremonies were believed necessary to propitiate the dieties who controlled rainfall and weather patterns as well as those other supernatural beings who inhabited plants, animals, and springs, and represented the world of the dead. The religion includes some five hundred of these spirits, and Indian artists evolved stylized representations of them. The figures appear as masks in tribal rituals and, more commonly,

as kachinas—small (four-to-sixteen-inch tall) figures of cottonwood, brightly painted and adorned with feathers and hair.

Kachina figures are designed in part as playthings for the children, but they are much more than that, for they also serve to instruct the young members of the tribe in their religious duties. For most whites, however, the main attraction of these figures is their powerful sculptural quality.

Kachinas have been collected since the 1880s, and fine collections exist in museums both here and abroad. Contemporary examples, though they are sometimes more self-consciously "arty" than the early pieces, often bring large sums, particularly if they are by a maker of some reputation. Works of lesser quality may be obtained through crafts and antiques dealers, but one should be aware of reproductions, in wood, plastic, or clay, which are made in Asia and frequently sold at tourist shops throughout the western states.

▲
Two well-made kachinas in polychromed wood, cloth, and feathers. *Left:* Wakak, or "cow kachina"; Zuni; 1915–25; $550–650. *Right:* Citota; Hopi; 1920–30; $350–425.

Bear dancer kachina in polychromed wood, cloth, dyed ▶ wool, and vegetable fiber; Zuni; 1910–25; $625–750. Nearly 1½′ tall, this is an important and appealing figure.

Early kachina in polychromed wood; $200–250. Though possibly dating to as early as the mid-19th century, this figure has lost portions of its body and most of its paint.
◀

◀
Unidentified kachina figure in polychromed wood, feathers, and cloth; Hopi; 1920–30; $450–550. Not all kachinas were made to resemble identifiable dieties.

Group of six small (4″) kachina figures in polychromed wood ▲ decorated in cloth and feathers; Hopi; 1925–35; $325–400 the set. Larger kachinas are usually of more interest to sophisticated collectors because fewer were made.

◀
Two kachinalike figures in polychromed wood; San Juan Pueblo, N.Mex.; ca. 1970; $125–145 each. The figure at right is the so-called water maiden.

Pottery

A great many American Indian groups have been making pottery since the craft was introduced here some 2,500 years ago. Prehistoric ceramics have been found from Maine to California, and these pieces are, of course, very much collectibles. However, most interest today centers on contemporary and late nineteenth–early twentieth-century ware from the pueblo area of the Southwest.

Such pueblos as Santa Clara, Acoma, and San Ildefonso produce high-quality ceramics. The Rancheria people, particularly the Yuma and Maricopa, also make some pieces, as do certain of the Navajo.

Southwestern pottery is distinguished both by its mode of manufacture and its style of decoration. Whereas most contemporary potters employ sophisticated gas or electric kilns and powered wheels, Indian potters work much as they did one hundred years ago. Disdaining the wheel, they build their ware on a coil. It is then polished smooth with a stone, colored where appropriate with mineral or vegetable dyes, and fired in a crude stone kiln or over an open fire. A black-hued body is achieved by smothering the fire in animal droppings, the so-called reduction method. The oxidation process used to create red and lighter-colored ware involves use of a fire with full access to oxygen.

The strong colors and geometric designs common to most pueblo pottery are immediately striking.

Though contemporary craftspeople have developed innovative adaptations, most of the decorative patterns emphasized reflect a tradition that goes back hundreds of years. It appears that when the first native potters began to decorate their work, they turned for inspiration to tribal basket makers, and now, countless generations later, potters are still employing variations of basketry-inspired motifs.

Pottery was originally functional, needed by the natives for everything from cooking and eating to the storage of raw materials and even the construction of toys and musical instruments. As factory-made goods proliferated, however, practical need diminished, until by the 1890s there was little real call for the craft. However, like rug and basket making, potting was saved by the development of a tourist market.

Interest in Indian ceramics has increased steadily over the past decades and is at present intense. A large quantity of contemporary ware comes out of the Southwest, and certain master potters like Maria Martinez and Tony Da are almost household words among knowledgeable collectors. Earlier ware is also in demand. Prices vary greatly. Large and elaborate works or those by renowned potters bring prices of hundreds or even thousands of dollars, while smaller, later, and more ordinary ware brings more modest prices.

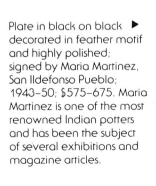

Plate in black on black ▶ decorated in feather motif and highly polished; signed by Maria Martinez, San Ildefonso Pueblo; 1943–50; $575–675. Maria Martinez is one of the most renowned Indian potters and has been the subject of several exhibitions and magazine articles.

Polished black on black ▲ pottery; San Ildefonso Pueblo. *Left:* Bowl; signed by Jeanette Martinez; 1940–55; $450–550. *Right:* Jar; signed by Maria and Julian Martinez; 1934–43; $600–700. The Martinez family is well known in contemporary potting circles, and their wares bring high prices.

◄

Polychrome ware; San Ildefonso Pueblo. *Left:* Double-lobed canteen in black and red on cream; 1950–51; $125–175. *Right:* Effigy pitcher in black on red; 1910–18; $400–500.

Left: Polychrome bowl in red and black on ▶ cream; San Ildefonso Pueblo; 1900–10; $235–285. *Right:* Water jar, or olla, in black on cream slip; Cochita Pueblo; 1950–60; $100–145.

Polychrome jar in black on white with bird and rain cloud motifs; Cochita Pueblo; 1895–1905; $1,200–1,400. This important piece of historic pottery reflects the characteristics of age and artistic merit sought by advanced collectors. ▼

Polished jar in red on red with well-executed dragon pattern; signed by Margaret Tofoya, Santa Clara Pueblo; 1960–70; $850–975. Among contemporary or near-contemporary pots, price differences (which may vary greatly for pieces from the same period and the same pueblo) usually reflect collector judgments as to artistic merit and desire for signed work by particular artisans. ◄

Polychrome pottery. *Left:* Bowl in black on red; Hopi; 1940–45; $185–245. *Right:* Bowl in red, tan, and cream; Santa Clara or San Juan pueblos; 1960–65; $75–100. ▼

◄

Polychrome pottery; Hopi Pueblo. *Left:* Small bowl in black on orange-white slip; 1945–53; $60–80. *Center:* Bowl in black on orange-white slip with bird motif; 1930–40; $265–345. *Right:* Vase in black and red on orange-white slip; 1970–74; $135–165.

Polychrome ceramic tiles; Hopi Pueblo; 1935–40. *Left:* Black and dark-brown slip on orange-white ground with bird motif; $110–140. *Center:* Kachina mask design in black and reddish-brown on orange-white; $90–120. *Right:* Kachina mask design in black and reddish-brown on orange-white base; $80–110. ▼

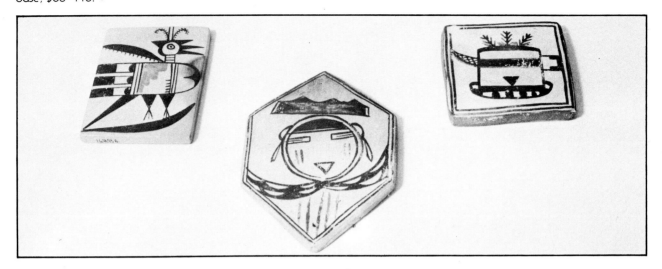

◄
Polychrome pottery in orange on tan; Mojave, Arizona; 1890–1900. *Left:* Small pitcher; $70–85. *Center:* Bowl; $180–250. *Right:* Cup; $90–115. The Mojave make a limited amount of pottery for their own use. It is seldom seen in contemporary collections.

Polychrome jar in black, red, and tan on white with parrot ▲ design; Acoma Pueblo; 1960–70; $265–355. Though not particularly well formed, this piece is nicely decorated.

◄

Polychrome
pottery; Acoma
Pueblo;
1960–70. *Left:*
Canteen in black
on white slip;
$75–100. *Center:*
Vase in
red-orange and
black on white;
$135–185. *Right:*
Small bowl in
brown on black
with red interior;
$50–65.

Well-decorated ►
polychrome
pottery in black
on red; Maricopa
Pueblo; 1950–65.
Left: Bowl;
$90–120. *Center:*
Bowl in white,
black, and red;
$115–160. *Right:*
Jar; $135–185.
Note how well
polished this ware
is, a sign of
painstaking
craftsmanship.

Polychrome pottery; Zuni; 1960–70. *Left:* Submarine-shape vessel (possibly a musical instrument) in red and cream slip; $50–65. *Top right:* Turtle-shape canteen in red, black, and cream slip; $90–115. *Bottom right:* Small pot with effigy handle in red and brown on yellowish-cream slip; $70–95. These pieces are cruder than most southwestern pottery. ▼

Polychrome pottery; Southwest. *Left:* Water jar in red and ▲ brown on white with traditional roadrunner motif; Zia; 1960–67; $200–260. Zia pottery is generally regarded as among the best fired of all southwestern ceramics. Unlike other pueblo ware, it will usually hold water. *Right:* Elaborately patterned plate in red, brown, and black on cream; Isleta Pueblo; 1965–67; $80–110.

Left: Cooking pot with single handle; San Juan Pueblo; ▲ 1940–50; $250–325. *Center:* Candlestick; Taos Pueblo; 1960–67; $55–70. *Right:* Large double-handled pot; San Lorenzo Pueblo; 1970–74; $160–220. Although from different pueblos, these pieces share a polished golden surface impregnated with mica, which makes it glisten.

Unusual Indian pottery. *Left:* Mug in black on white slip; ▲ Southwest; 1960–70; $35–45. *Center:* Pot in reddish-brown slip; Southwest; $60–75. *Right:* Pot in cream slip decorated with tooled "rope cord" markings, a decorative technique employed by the earliest Indian potters; Hopi Pueblo; 1960–70; $75–100.

Basketry

The basket-making tradition in North America is ancient, and its origins are lost in unrecorded history. It is certain, however, that the art and craft of basketry was being practiced in many areas of what is now the United States as early as the birth of Christ. Most of what was made then is now lost, of course, and contemporary collectors focus on Indian baskets made after 1880.

The most sought after of these receptacles are those produced in the West, where nomadic tribes needed light, durable carrying and storage containers, and where roots and grasses suitable for their manufacture existed in abundance. So important was basketry in the ancient Southwest that the ancestors of the Pueblo Indians were known as "the basket makers."

It is generally agreed that the center of collectible baskets is California, followed by the Southwest, and then the Northwest Coast. In a sense such distinctions are meaningless, for basketry is a very individual craft. Although Apache baskets in general are characterized by swirling motifs and those of the Papago by the utilization of complex geometric designs, the manner in which each individual piece is executed is the real test. As in every other area of crafts, there are good basket makers and ones who are not so good.

Collectors use various criteria for determining the quality and value of baskets. Age is certainly important. Because of their fragile nature, few baskets exceed a century in age, so even an example from circa 1900 is rare. But even more important are aesthetic considerations, such as how well the piece is made and decorated, how suitable the material chosen is to the shape and method of weaving employed. Condition, too, is a factor. While there are few "perfect" baskets, extensive damage seriously devalues a piece.

Storage baskets are the most common type of basket, but many other forms can be found, such as trays, bowls, plates, strainers, burden baskets, cradles, hats, and even special containers in which grasshoppers were cooked! Unusual forms and sizes (baskets range in size from thimble size to ten feet tall) are regarded as most desirable.

Coiled basketry; Southwest. *Left:* Bowl made for Navajo use in the so-called Navajo wedding-basket design in red, brown, and tan; Paiute; 1970–73; $65–85. *Right:* Pitcher in yellow and brown on cream; 1965–70; $70–95.

◀

Burden basket in tan and brown; Apache; 1945–60; $300–375. These containers were carried on the back and supported by a band across the carrier's forehead. ▼

Basketry water jars, or ollas; Apache. *Left:* Dark tan with ▲ leather shoulder thong; 1900–10; $600–700. *Right:* Light tan with cloth thong; 1930–40; $450–550. Water jars are tightly woven; their interiors are coated with pitch.

Basketry water jars. ▶
Left: Bottle-shape jar; Ute; 1920–30; $115–140. *Right:* Olla with handle of braided horsehair; Walapai; 1910–25; $260–320. These jars are coated inside and out with pitch from the Pinon pine. Water jars are not common.

Polychrome coiled basketry. *Left:* Covered box in black and tan in frog design; Pima; 1940–50; $175–245. *Center:* Double-handled basket in tan and cream; Papago; 1960–65; $45–55. *Right:* Coiled basketry plaque in brown and cream; Apache; 1960–65; $160–210.

Left: Tray in dark brown on tan with strong geometric pattern; Pima; 1930–40; $240–290. *Center:* Basket in black on tan; Papago; 1920–30; $90–125. *Right:* Bowl in dark brown on tan; Pima; 1930–40; $230–280. ▼

Coiled covered basket in natural split rush; Ute; 1910–30; ▶
$200–250. The plain, undecorated surface of this basket is in
sharp contrast to most southwestern examples.

Coiled circular baskets in cream, dark brown, and yellow;
Hopi; 1930–45. *Left:* Handled in sawtooth pattern; $65–85.
Center: With stylized animal motifs; $185–225. *Right:* With
geometric decoration, missing handle; $95–135. Figural
decoration generally enhances the value of a piece. ▼

Basketry; Mono; ▶
1910–30. *Top:* Finely
woven parching or
drying tray in black on
tan with interesting
zigzag pattern;
$145–195. *Bottom:*
Seed beater used in
food preparation;
$55–75.

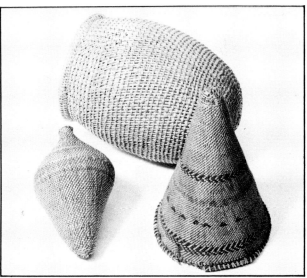

▲
Left: Pear-shaped seed or water bottle in tan willow; Mono;
1920–35; $70–95. *Center:* Rare cooking basket used in the
preparation of grasshoppers; Bannock; 1910–20; $175–225.
Right: Burden basket in black and red on tan in geometric
pattern; Mono; 1910–25; $210–260.

◀

Glass vessels covered with woven basketry. *Left:* Food jar in
black and brown on tan in geometric pattern; Paiute;
1958–60; $80–110. *Center:* Wine bottle in black and tan; Pit
River Indians; 1960–70; $135–170. *Right:* Shallow food jar
with cover in brown and tan; Northwest Coast; 1920–30;
$160–220.

51

Basketry; Northwest Coast. *Left:* Basket banded in dark brown on tan; Lost River (Modoc); 1905–07; $75–100. *Center:* Shallow strainer in light and dark tan; Klamath; 1910–25; $65–90. *Right:* Looped-rim basket in brown and purple; Quinault; 1920–30; $90–115.

Left: Small bowl in black and yellow; Pit River Indians; 1910–20; $100–125. *Center:* Large basket in black and yellow on pale yellow with bold geometric design; Pit River Indians; 1910–20; $245–295. *Right:* Covered box in red, brown, and tan; Makah; 1950–60; $65–90. The excellent weave of these baskets is typical of the Northwest Coast.
◀

Burden basket in light cream on tan; Klamath River Indians; 1900–10; $600–700. The excellent decoration and fine weave of this piece mark it as the work of a master craftsman. ▼

Cradle in woven roots; Oregon Coast; 1920–30; $135–185. Basketry cradles are relatively uncommon, most having been destroyed through use. ▶

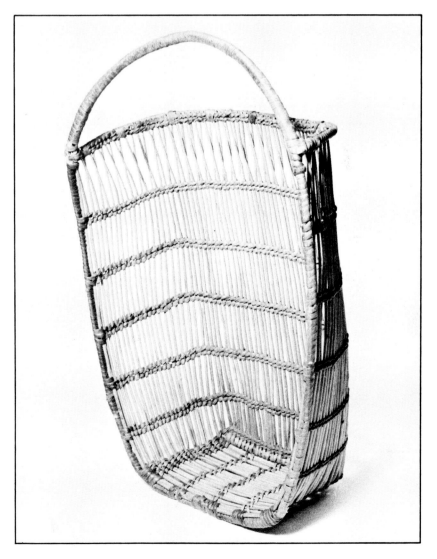

Octagonal double-handled cedar root basket in red and tan; Salish; 1950–60; $45–55. The shape of this basket is rare among Indian baskets. ▶

Bowl in brown on tan with geometric pattern; Pima; 1920–25; $140–180. The excellent condition of this piece is a plus with collectors, the majority of whom reject seriously damaged basketry. ▼

Finely woven jar in dark brown on tan with geometric ▲
pattern; Pima; 1915–25; $400–500. Containers of this sort
were often used to store corn and various grains.

The Bluecoats

Of all the romantic figures who people the mythical West, few compare with the blue-coated cavalryman. Over the decades, thousands of children (and adults) have risen screaming from their theater seats as the bugle sounds and, in a cloud of dust, the cavalry sweeps to the aid of the beleaguered fort or wagon train. Such events did occur, but they were relatively rare. Far more frequently the wily red men had done their work and stolen far away before the weary troopers slogged across the horizon. They would go after the malefactors, and usually they got them. In most cases the bluecoats caught the Indians while they slept or in the dead of winter, for the Indians were notoriously lax about posting guards and did not regard winter as a proper time for fighting.

The weapons used by the cavalry and infantrymen in the Indian Wars are highly collectible. Enthusiasts also seek uniforms, caps, hats, and accessories such as belt buckles and boots. Because most of these items were general issue and manufactured in the thousands, it is usually not too difficult to amass a collection. It is, however, often quite hard (lacking an authenticated history) to ascertain that a particular piece was used against the Indians.

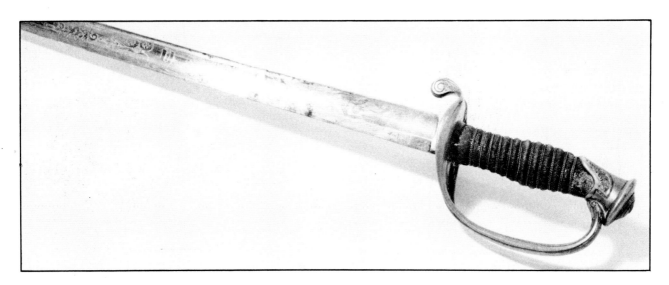

Detail of hilt and upper blade of U.S. Army iron and steel cavalry officer's sword; said to ▲ have been used in Arizona; 1875–85; $175–235.

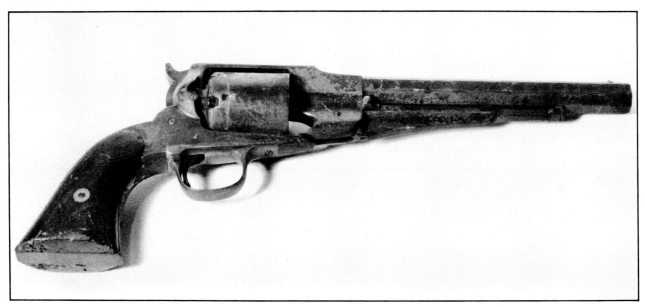

U.S. Army percussion-type .44-caliber revolver; $175–200. First used during the ▲ Civil War, the heavy but accurate ''forty-four'' was the standard military sidearm in the West until well into the 1880s. It was carried by both officers and enlisted men.

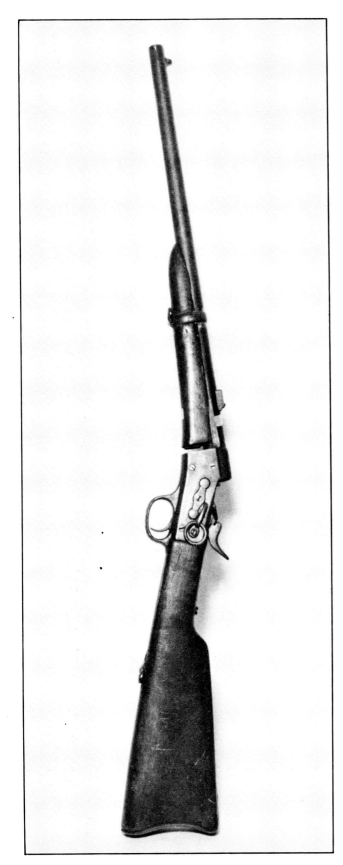

U.S. Army cavalryman's belt buckle in brass; 1870–90; ▲ $65–80. Brass buckles, buttons, and other military accoutrements are very popular with some collectors because they are both attractive and easy to display and store.

▲
U.S. Army fatigue caps of the sort used by troops in the West. *Left:* Kepi in blue wool; 1880–90; $135–155. *Right:* Standard undress cap in blue wool; 1890–1900; $50–65.

◄

U.S. Army .44-caliber cavalry rolling-block carbine; by Remington; 1890–95; $180–220. The carbine was essential to the cavalryman. The standard rifle issued to foot soldiers was far too long to be carried with comfort or used effectively on horseback.

2.

The Spanish Colonists

Only recently have collectors outside the immediate area had an opportunity to view and acquire the antiques and folk art associated with the Spanish-speaking peoples of the American Southwest, yet that culture is one of the oldest on this continent.

It was in 1536, a century before major settlement began in New England, that wandering Spanish soldiers brought back tales of legendary wealth in an area far to the north of Mexico City, at that time the most distant outpost of the empire. The Seven Cities of Cibola, as they were called, were said to be roofed in gold and to contain a vast wealth of precious metals. After several abortive expeditions, the renowned Francisco Coronado reached the cities in 1540, following a grim march across the wastes of New Mexico. What he found was disappointing: the mud- and stone-walled dwellings of the Zuni Indians. There was no gold and no silver.

Not too surprisingly the Spanish left the area to its native inhabitants for the next half-century. But the rumors of wealth persisted. Perhaps the fabled cities existed somewhere else in the vast and unknown North. Between 1581 and 1593, no fewer than five expeditions explored what is now New Mexico and Arizona (these states and Colorado and Texas were known as New Mexico under the Spanish). Then, in 1598, the first serious efforts to colonize the area were made, followed by the founding, in 1610, of Santa Fe.

From then on the Spanish gradually extended their control over the territory. Ranchers and small farmers arrived from Mexico, and missions were established for the education and conversion of the Indians. They, however, proved ungrateful to their new masters, and during the Pueblo Rebellion of 1680, killed off or drove out most of the new settlers.

Time and the tides of history were running against the Navajo and Zuni, and by the mid-1690s the white men had returned in greater numbers and had once more subjugated their reluctant hosts.

Things did not go well in the new lands. They were

so far from the main Spanish strongholds that it was difficult to supply and protect them. Though the sedentary cliff dwellers were subjugated, the warlike Apache harried the colonists constantly, and from the north came a new threat, marauding Plains Indians newly mounted on stolen Spanish horses. Moreover, by the early 1700s there were rumors of French settlements on the Missouri, an area the Iberians had thought of as their eastern frontier. These stories were soon proved to be fact as French traders began to appear in Santa Fe during the 1720s, and until they withdrew, following the conclusion of the French and Indian War, the French posed a constant threat to New Spain.

In the meantime, the colonists were not inactive. They built mills, brought in stock, and opened crude roads for the rough two-wheeled wagons, known as carretas, that were their principle form of transportation. Mounted on horses and mules, they forged west until, in 1776, the Franciscan priest Francisco Garces breached the mountains and deserts and linked New Mexico by land with the Spanish colony in California. In the years that followed, hundreds of traders followed the Spanish Trail from Santa Fe to Pueblo de Los Angeles.

The land now held by the Spanish was immeasurably vast and almost incredibly rich, but the conquerors' grasp proved too weak to maintain it. Spanish power declined throughout the New World, and soon after 1800, rebellions, cast in the mold of the American Revolution, flared in many areas of the empire. Mexico was not immune, and, in 1821, its leaders declared their independence.

This had a profound effect on New Mexico. The revolutionary government, even weaker and more impoverished than its predecessor, could do little for its northern territories. The trickle of priests, supplies, and culture from the south ground to a halt. New Mexico was left to its own devices.

There were others eager to supply what the compesinos were lacking. American traders had been aware of New Mexico for some time, and as demand for furs, particularly bison skins, increased, they began to filter into the area. At first they came by horse or even on foot, but in 1822, the first wagon trains rumbled into Santa Fe. The new arrivals liked what they saw. The land was sparsely populated (no more than 26,000 persons in the whole territory), mineral wealth was evident, there were herds of bison, and, most important, the possibilities of grazing and farming seemed limitless.

During the late 1820s and the early 1830s, thousands of Americans poured into New Mexico, gradually displacing its former inhabitants and gaining control of its riches. Mexico, weak as it was, had to react, and it did with the fatal assault on the Alamo. Thereafter, the land's fate was sealed. The Republic of Texas arose, the Mexican army was crushed in the Mexican War of 1846–1848, and by the Treaty of Guadalupe, all of New Mexico was ceded to the United States. New Spain had ceased to exist.

This did not end the Spanish-American culture of the Southwest. Quite the contrary. Though driven into the poorer areas and largely forgotten by their conquerors, the Iberian herders and farmers survived and preserved what was theirs. This, essentially, was their church and the arts and practices that had grown up around it.

No immigrants to these shores were more church oriented than the Spanish, and it is not possible to talk of their arts and crafts without being aware of the religious context. New Mexican painting and sculpture is almost entirely religious in inspiration and execution. The way the people lived (and still do live) in small, isolated towns built up about a church reflects the importance of that institution in their lives.

Moreover, isolation and poverty are often good defenses against cultural change. There was little in the mountain villages of New Mexico to interest the newcomers, so for generations the people were left to paint and carve religious figurines to grace their chapels, and to be used in religious festivities; to shape from soft pine and cottonwood the simple tables, chests, and chairs with which they furnished their crude homes; and to weave the lovely textiles for which the area is so well known. Even as late as the 1900s, the technique and substance of this work had changed surprisingly little.

Unfortunately, when change did come, it came with a rush. First to be affected was the religious art, with plaster figurines and mass-produced lithographs sounding the death knell for most folk painters and carvers. Then came cheap blankets and sheets to put an end to weaving, and Grand Rapids furniture to replace locally constructed pieces, which in style had retained the look and feel of the seventeenth century.

As they were replaced, the old things were often discarded, and were it not for the efforts of farsighted museum personnel and a few collectors, all might have been lost. But now those few who struggled through the 1920s and 1930s to salvage some small part of this great heritage have been joined by a multitude. Collecting New Mexican artifacts is ``in,'' at least in the Southwest, and prices for santos, furniture, leatherwork, iron, silver, and textiles are soaring. The empire has been, in some sense, regained.

Furniture and Furnishings

Isolated as they were from the mainstream of Spanish colonial culture, the settlers in Arizona, Texas, New Mexico, and California were required, for the most part, to manufacture their own furniture and household implements. Because the pioneers were of Hispanic background, these objects reflected the styles and tastes of Iberia and its major colonial outposts such as Mexico City and Guadalajara. However, the lack of trained artisans, particularly after Mexico gained its independence, and the need to use locally available raw materials led to great culture lag. This is very noticeable in furniture making: chairs and chests dating to the midnineteenth century were crafted in a style that had prevailed in Spain two hundred years before. The sort of stylistic progression (from Queen Anne to Chippendale to Federal) so common in the eastern United States never existed in the Spanish areas of the Southwest.

The poverty and limited resources of the colonists, who were almost continually beset by hostile Indians and a hostile environment, never allowed for much furniture, and few forms other than tables, chairs, chests, and cupboards are to be found. Most of these are of pine or cottonwood and date to the 1800s. The artisans that made them are for the most part unknown, for it was not customary to sign one's work. There are, however, exceptions to this rule. Several pieces, for example, can be traced to Manuel Archuleta, a cabinetmaker who was active in Taos, New Mexico, 1850–60.

Iberians have always been great metal workers, excelling especially in the shaping of iron, and wrought or cast objects in this medium are among the most interesting things found in the Southwest. Furniture hardware, such as locks, latches, hinges, and the like, are often elaborately shaped and decorated with punchwork, twisting, and engraving. Also seen are finely wrought spurs; iron crosses for churches, homes, and graveyards; and a great variety of cast- and wrought-iron fencing and grillwork.

Though expensive—it was not available locally and had to be traded for—tin also was used extensively, particularly in the manufacture of household cooking ware, lighting devices, and religious items such as crosses and the mirrored boxes in which statues of saints were exhibited.

Leather was available in substantial quantity both from the herds of wandering buffalo and from domestic stock, so the Spanish tradition of fine leatherwork was also continued. Beautifully formed and decorated saddles, bridles, gloves, and even boxes were made for local use and for barter with the hardy traders who followed the long and dangerous trail to Santa Fe.

During the past decade, collectors, particularly in the southwestern states, have become more aware of the beauty and significance of Spanish-American furniture and household accessories, and steps have been taken to preserve what is left. Unfortunately, this aid has come too late for many objects never made in large quantity and for too many years scorned by Anglo and Hispanic alike as crude and old-fashioned. These precious bits of past heritage have all too often been lost.

Trastero, or cupboard; New Mexico; mid-19th century; $6,000–7,500. Based on a traditional Spanish design, these storage pieces are found throughout Central and South America. Unfortunately, few authenticated southwestern examples have survived. ▼

Table in pine; Taos, N.Mex.; 1830–60; $650–850. Tables such as this were found in many southwestern homes, where they provided a work surface as well as a storage area. ▼

◄
Side chair in pine; by Manuel Archuleta; Taos, N.Mex.; 1850–60; $450–550. Manuel Archuleta is one of the few identified Hispanic cabinetmakers. The sharply angular lines and shallow, simple carving are typical of furniture made in Spain during the 17th century.

Pair of polychromed wall brackets in red, yellow, and black; early 20th century; $275–350. Intended as decorative pieces, these brackets would have been regarded as a luxury in most Spanish-American homes. ▼

Fencing in wrought and cast iron; New Mexico; 1900–10; ▲ $200–300. Intended for protection as well as admired for its beauty, ironwork was found on or about most houses and is available today in quantity.

Ladles in wrought iron; late 19th century. *Left:* $60–75. *Right:* $90–110. In most cases, the more ornate a piece of iron, the greater its value. ▼

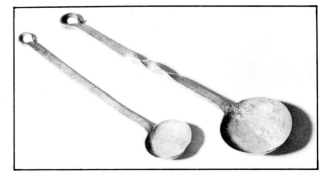

Cross in wrought iron; northern New Mexico; 1910–20; ▲ $300–375. The Spanish tradition of working in iron lingered in the Southwest, and even during this century iron crosses were a common sight at crossroads and in churchyards.

Chandelier in tin; Honda Mora, N.Mex.; 1890–1910; ▶
$600–700. Decorated with punchwork and cut-tin hearts, this
lighting device is a true piece of folk art.

Spurs in wrought iron; Texas and Arizona; 1890–1910;
$125–175. No one made more elaborate spurs and iron- ·
mounted horse bridles than the Spanish artisans of the Southwest, and such items were being offered to eastern traders
before 1850. ▼

Candle lantern ▶
in tin;
1880–1900;
$165–210. This
piece is
decorated
with a sunburst
pattern
produced by
piercing the
metal with a
sharp
instrument.

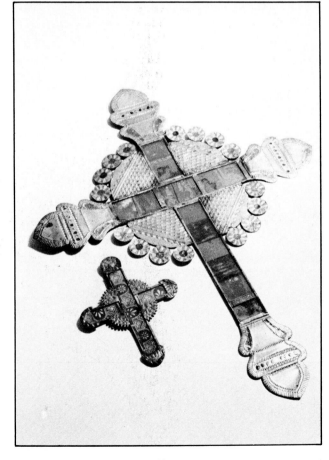

Crosses in tin and glass. *Left:* Brown glass; $75–100 *Right:* Red and green ▲
glass; $160–200. Pieces such as this were typically hung in bedrooms or
in the part of the house set aside as a family shrine.

Unusual polychrome geometric candleholder in yellow and black; Hondo, N.Mex.; 1885–95; $150–200. The strong, contrasting colors and sharp angles of this piece may reflect Indian influences. ▼

Storage box in rawhide and leather inset with red ▲ flannel and blue velvet; New Mexico; 1870–85; $200–275. This beautifully crafted receptacle was probably intended for a woman's valuables.

◄ Powder bottle in rawhide with decorative stitched pattern; New Mexico; 1880–1900; $135–165. The stopper is of carved wood.

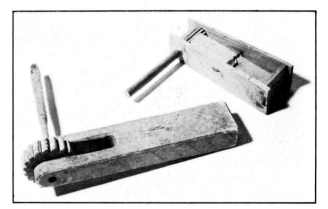

Noisemakers, or clackers, in wood; Southwest; ▲ 1920–35; $45–60. These were used in religious ceremonies of the Penitente cult.

Saddle in ► tooled leather; Southwest; 1910–30; $350–450. The leather-workers of the Spanish-speaking communities made many of the saddles used in the western states.

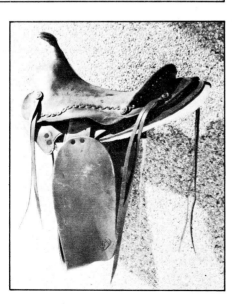

Reconstructed ▶
chapel of shrine of
Our Lady of Talpa;
Talpa, N.Mex.;
1840–1900.
Salvaged and
accurately
reconstructed, this
typical New Mexican
village church is now
on display at the
Taylor Museum in
Colorado Springs,
Colo.

Santos

The folk sculpture and painting produced by the Spanish-speaking people of the southwestern United States is almost exclusively religious in nature, a fact that sets it apart from the folk art produced in other parts of the country. This situation is a reflection of the nature of the Spanish colonial government and the artist's role in relation to that government.

Unlike other American pioneers who came to settle in and develop the new country, the Spanish came for gold and souls. Their troops sought to wrest precious metals from the Indians, while the accompanying priests attempted to convert the suddenly destitute heathen. Religious images associated with the Christian faith played a major role in both over-awing and converting the native populace. Paintings and sculpture proved potent tools in overcoming the language barrier, while religious images in every church and town kept a sharp eye on those who might be tempted to transgress Spanish rule.

The new missions and churches needed painting and sculpture, but the demand for such works was even more widespread. The Spanish had traditionally had village and even family saints, and those who came to the new world continued this tradition. In accessible areas of the empire, this need for imagery could be filled by pieces brought from Europe or created by European academic painters and sculptors. But there were few professionals in New Mexico and California, and European works of art seldom found their way up the long trail from Mexico. Therefore those who aspired to paint or carve found their services in demand.

The untrained men who produced the folk painting and sculpture of the Southwest were known as *santeros* (``painters of saints''), and their works were known as *santos*. There are two distinct types of santos: *bultos*, which are carved figures; and *retablos*, painted wooden panels. Both usually depict individual saints or groups of saints.

Bultos are traditionally carved in the round from cottonwood or soft pine, coated with a layer of white plasterlike gesso, and painted in bright tempera colors. Depending on the maker's skill and inclinations, a bulto might be whittled from a single piece of wood; from several, with arms, feet, or hands doweled or glued on; or a bulto can consist of a carved bust with open framework base covered in gesso-stiffened fabric.

Retablos are painted pictures on gesso-coated pine panels. They vary from tiny four-inch-square pieces used in home altars to large groups of linked panels, known as *reredos*, which served as altar screens in churches.

Although there were santeros at work from the earliest days of Spanish colonization, the great bulk of the existing santos dates from 1820–1900. Before 1820, Spanish priests greatly influenced santero work both through their own carving and painting and through the prints and paintings that they brought with them from Europe or Mexico City. After 1900, the introduction of cheap lithographs and plaster figures cut sharply into the santeros' business.

The greatest santos were produced during the period when New Mexico and the surrounding area were ignored by both the impoverished Mexican government and the United States. Lacking outside sources of inspiration, the artists were thrown back upon their own resources. Their work took on a stark simplicity very much suited to the land in which it was produced. Bodies grew long and slender; hands, feet, and heads became disproportionately large in relation to bodies. Top hats and other elements of nineteenth-century western clothing replaced the figures' classical robes. The santos became a distinct regional form of folk art, unlike anything else found in the United States.

As is so often the case, by the time collectors discovered santos, they were already vanishing, taking with them much of the oral and written tradition that would have made it possible to identify the santeros. Fortunately, some of these carvers and painters are known—at least by their works.

In some cases the santeros signed their creations. The New Mexican retablo painter José Rafael Aragón (ca. 1830–1850) is a case in point. However, most santeros were itinerant, and they rarely put their names to their work. A few works can be identified by their style or by the initials of their creators, such as the well-known AJ santero of New Mexico. Signed or not, bultos and retablos are increasingly popular collectors' items.

The art did not die out completely at the end of the nineteenth century. Men such as José Dolores Lopez of Cordova, New Mexico, continued to work into the present era, and their work is now eagerly sought not by humble peasants and rural padres but by museums and private collectors. Unfortunately, this revival seems to have been limited to carving. Comparable retablo makers have not appeared.

▲
Dolores figure; New Mexico; 1880–1900; $900–1,200. This figure of the grieving mother consists of a carved cottonwood torso mounted on a stickwork frame over which gesso-coated linen has been stretched. The predominant colors are blue and pink.

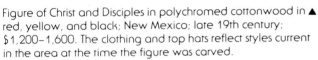

Figure of Christ and Disciples in polychromed cottonwood in ▲ red, yellow, and black; New Mexico; late 19th century; $1,200–1,600. The clothing and top hats reflect styles current in the area at the time the figure was carved.

Manger with figure of San Ysidro in polychromed wood; ▶ New Mexico; 1870–90; $750–900. Painted in yellow, black, green, and white, this composition is particularly vivid and striking.

Life-size figure of Christ in polychromed cottonwood; Chapel of Our Lady of Talpa, Talpa, N.Mex.; ca. 1840; $15,000–20,000. This extremely important piece is attributed to the santero José Rafael Aragon. ▼

Nazarene Christ in polychromed wood, horsehair, and cloth; northern New Mexico; mid-19th century; $1,250–1,500. Christ figures, some nearly life-size, were carried in processions conducted by the Penitente Brotherhood during Holy Week ceremonies. ▼

Nazarene Christ in polychromed wood, horsehair, and cloth; northern New Mexico; 1850–60; $3,500–4,200. New Mexican folk sculpture is almost entirely religious in nature and, understandably, bears a close resemblance to Mexican work—with which it is often confused.

◄

Storage chest in pine with red paint and wrought-iron lock and hinges and dovetailing; New Mexico; 1860–80; $175–250. There is relatively little remaining New Mexican furniture. What can be found consists primarily of chairs, tables, and chests. ▼

Crosses; 1890–1920. *Left:* Notch carved; $145–175. *Right:* ▲ Straw-work decorated; $85–110. These are typical of the crosses found in many homes.

◄ *Nicho,* or "saint's house," in polychromed cottonwood; New Mexico; early 20th century; $375–450. Such objects were used to display holy figures.

Nino de Atocha retablo in ▲ polychromed pine; 1870–90; $1,800–2,000. Painted in red, green, gray, black, and brown, this tempera panel probably once hung in a private chapel.

Retablo of San Juan Nomucene in ▲ polychromed pine; late 19th century; $1,500–1,800. Prayers were offered to images of this type at the time of family illness, natural disaster, or on Holy Days.

Retablo of Santa Getrude in red, ▲ white, and black tempera on pine panel; New Mexico; 1880–1900; $1,600–1,900. Though once rather common, good-quality retablos are fast vanishing from the market.

Holy family in red, brown, black, and tan tempera on tin; 1880–1900; $650–750. Like many retablos, this one was probably copied from a religious print. ◄

Face of Christ ► in tempera on tin plate; New Mexico; 1870–1900; $550–700. Though more commonly of Mexican origin, painted-tin retablos of American origin are known.

Family, or roadside, shrine in glass and polychromed tin; ▲ New Mexico; 1900–10; $450–550. This representation of *Nino de Atocha* forms part of the small decorated shrine found in every Spanish-American home.

Decorated shrine in tin and glass; 1910–25; $200–250. ► Elaborately decorated shrines such as this were often made in small tinsmiths' shops.

▲
Retablo in tempera on board; by the Santo Nino santero;
Chimayo, N.Mex.; 1830–40; $1,100–1,400. The figure is the
Mater Dolores, a popular subject with religious artists.

◄ Polychromed altar piece in wood; Tucumcari, N.Mex.;
1880–1900; $1,500–2,000. Because many old village
churches have been destroyed, few such altar pieces remain.

Bulto of the *Santa Familia* in polychromed wood; by Fray ▲
Andres Garcia; 1780–85; $2,000–2,500. Bultos have been
produced in New Mexico since the 17th century. The names
of a few sculptors, such as Garcia's, are known to collectors.

75

Retablo of San Juan Nomucene in tempera on board; ▲
northern New Mexico; 1820–30; $1,750–2,000. This work is
by the ''AJ'' santero, so-called because some of his retablos
are initialed AJ. Signed retablos are much sought after.

Textiles

A locally based textile industry was of great importance to the New Mexican settlers, both for their own use and for trade with Anglos and Indians. Indigenous tribes, particularly the Navajo, had woven cotton and other vegetable fibers for hundreds of years, but introduction of sheep by the Spanish opened new vistas in textiles.

Every Spanish colonial home had a spinning wheel for spinning yarn and one or more crude hardwood or pine looms with which to weave bedding, carpets, and clothing. The looms used in the Southwest were narrow, horizontal harness machines that turned out narrow strips of woolen cloth no more than twenty-six inches wide. These were characteristically sewn together to create wider blankets and floor coverings. Various types of weaving—diamond, herringbone, and diagonal—were employed.

Until about 1860, all yarn was hand spun from wool prepared on the farm and was colored with natural dyes made from roots, clay, bark, or lichen. Colors were, accordingly, muted, and patterns were few, chiefly stripes and lozenges. Following the introduction, in the 1860s, of bright commercial dyes and Germantown yarns, it became possible for weavers to create a wide variety of new patterns.

As the twentieth century dawned, the Spanish weaving tradition gradually vanished in most areas as homemade textiles were replaced by cheaper factory-made material. However, in the Chimayo Valley not far from Santa Fe, New Mexico, weavers carried on, gradually adapting their work to appeal to tourists and collectors rather than local customers. This Chimayo tradition still persists as the last remnant of a craft that once flourished from the Mexican border to Colorado.

Although shawls, mattress ticking, and floor coverings (jerga) were woven, blankets are by far the most popular Spanish-American textiles. These were used both as bedding and as cloaks. The cloaks served the same function as the Mexican serape, from which they may be distinguished by their lack of a center slit for the head. Confusion with the somewhat-similar blankets of the southwestern Indians can be avoided by remembering certain differences in pattern and weaving, particularly the fact that colonial examples were made of two pieces sewn together.

An unusual variation was embroidery in wool on a woven-wool ground. This work was characterized by the colcha stitch, a long stitch anchored by diagonal holding stitches. Pieces so designed were sometimes completely covered with embroidery.

Above all, collectors prize the embroidered bed covers (also known as colcha) made from the 1840s on and highlighted by elaborate floral motifs and wavy scalloping. Such designs often have a distinctly oriental quality, a fact that leads to speculation that they may be derived from Asiatic textiles imported through the Spanish colony in the Philippines. Another possible source for the design is old Mexico, where similar patterns, but not the colcha stitch, are found. Whichever, explanation is correct, embroidered wool work is both prized and scarce.

Blanket in woven wool in blue, white, and brown zigzag ▲ pattern; Chimayo region, N.Mex.; 1870–90; $675–775. The tradition of home weaving has lasted longest in the Chimayo Valley north of Santa Fe.

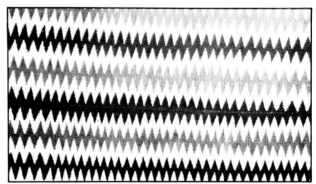

Detail of blanket in woven wool in vertical tan, blue, and ▲ brown design; New Mexico; 1900–20; $600–700.

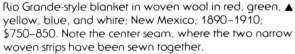

Rio Grande-style blanket in woven wool in red, green, ▲ yellow, blue, and white; New Mexico; 1890–1910; $750–850. Note the center seam, where the two narrow woven strips have been sewn together.

Blanket in woven wool in yellow and purple; New Mexico; 20th century; $250–300. This interesting figural blanket is typical of pieces woven for the collector and tourist. ▶

Mater Dolores retablo in tempera on ▲
board; by José Aragon; New Mexico;
early 19th century; $900–1,200.
Retablos and bultos have generally
been slighted by collectors and art
historians more familiar with New
England-style folk art. They are,
however, an important area of
American craftsmanship.

San José in polychromed wood; by ▶
Felix Lopez; San Jose, N.Mex.; 20th
century; $750–850. Lopez's work is in
the Museum of New Mexico and the
Museum of American Folk Art. He is
regarded as one of the leading
santeros.

San Antonio and Santa Rita in polychromed wood; Taos,
N.Mex.; 1850–65; $1,700–2,000 the pair. Earlier santos are
more desirable than those carved in the 20th century.
However, workmanship and artistic expression are the major
keys to value.

Small dome-top storage chest in pine inlaid with straw work;
Santa Fe, N.Mex.; 1880–1910; $150–200. Straw workers
have practiced their art in Santa Fe for decades.

Blanket in woven wool in ▶
red, green, brown, and
black; Chimayo region,
N.Mex.; mid-20th century;
$300–400. Note the
resemblance of the central
figure to some seen on
retablos.

Shawl in woven wool
brocaded white on deep
purple; New Mexico; 20th
century; $175–250. Shawls
like this are another
popular tourist item in both
old and New Mexico. ▼

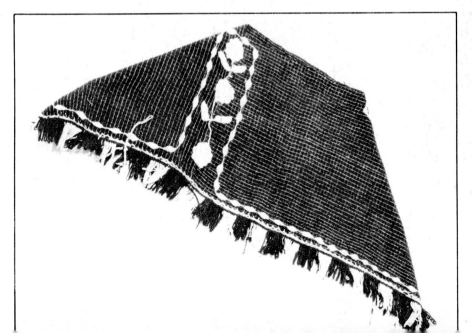

Homespun bed cover in embroidered wool on wool with decorative design in the colcha stitch; New Mexico; late 19th century; $850–950. Predominate colors are red, brown, blue, and yellow. ▼

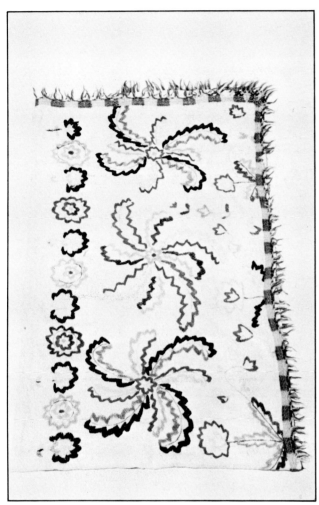

Colcha bed cover; New Mexico; 1870–80; $1,000–1,300. ▲ The bold colors (blue, brown, and white) and exciting geometric design make this colcha a ''must'' for the collector.

Embroidered ▶ colcha, or bed cover, in the sabanilla manner; New Mexico; 1870–90; $850–950. In sabanillas elements of the design are less formalized and more of the ground is left exposed.

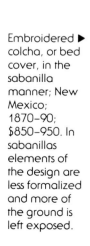

Embroidered colcha in wool on cotton in red, brown, ▲ yellow, and blue; 1870–90; $700–800. In certain areas of the Southwest, cotton rather than wool was used as ground for embroidery. The term *sabanilla* is frequently applied to bed covers made in this manner.

3.

Mountain Men and Buffalo Runners

Though they founded no cities, built no railroads, dug no mines, and usually died poor, the early trappers and hunters left an indelible mark on the American West. From Seattle to Houston the rivers and ridges bear their names, and American folklore is richer for their exploits.

Americans were not the first to brave the mountains and deserts of the West and to fall in love with its wildlife and wilder inhabitants. First were the *coureurs de bois*, or "woods runners," French explorers and traders so hardy that they were commonly said to have bodies of brass, eyes of glass, and blood flowing in brandy. Before 1700 these men had penetrated the Rockies and visited Santa Fe, defying the officials of two nations—their own, which outlawed them for violating the government monopoly on fur trading; and that of Spain, which saw them as the advance guard of Gallic imperialism.

The *coureurs* were tough and adaptable. They adopted Indian dress and customs and even took Indian wives, a social transgression in the eyes of their more staid fellows, who branded them forever as "squaw men." But flexible as they were, they could not survive the system that had spawned them, and when, in 1764, France ceded its North American colony to England, they passed from the scene.

In their place came the British in Canada and, below the border, the Americans. Pushing ever westward, these early American adventurers disregarded the nominal Spanish title to the western fastnesses. In 1805, when Lewis and Clark reached the Pacific Coast on foot, they were surprised to find their fellow citizens trapping beaver along the remote Yellowstone River.

The beaver were very important. These little animals, whose skins were highly prized as headgear in Europe, were thick in the mountains, and it was not long before groups of men organized to trade for pelts with the Indians living along the Missouri River, the main avenue of access to the unsettled regions. Among the first of these entrepreneurs was John Colter, who had traveled with Lewis and Clark. Colter soon found out that fur trading was not all profit.

Caught in the open by hostile Blackfeet, he was stripped of his clothing and given a chance to run for his life. The Indians no doubt anticipated a brief chase, but the trappers were robust men. Colter gradually outdistanced all but one of his pursuers, and when this brave fell while attempting to cast his spear, the unarmed mountain man killed him with his own weapon. Then, alone and naked in the wilderness, the trapper walked seven days to reach an outpost, subsisting on roots and berries.

There were many others like Colter, and not all of them escaped their red-skinned foes. Still, they came, lured on by the wealth of beaver and the lure of the wild. By 1820 their number had grown so large that they took to doing their own trapping rather than buying Indian furs. And when, in 1822, one of the major fur companies decided to hire trappers as private contractors rather than wage workers, the mountain men were born.

These "free trappers" sold their catch to the companies at half the eastern price, a lot of money in those days. They were beholden to no one, their lives and luck depending on their own skill. During the 1820s they swarmed through the western mountains seeking their elusive prey. It was they who opened the Santa Fe Trail, making possible the exploitation of the fur-bearing wealth of the southern Rockies. One of their number, Jedediah S. Smith, crossed the Sierra at Yosemite and reached the Spanish colony at San Diego. He caused the authorities there no little anxiety, and brought back what he sought—Sierra beaver pelts.

The development of free trapping also led to the establishment of the legendary Rocky Mountain Rendezvous. In 1825 one of the fur barons, William Ashley, decided that the only way to reach all the widely scattered men he employed was to meet them at one designated spot in the mountains. Accordingly, he made arrangements to bring his supply train (money was useless in the wild, so payment for the furs was made in goods) to Utah's Green River in July of that year.

The new arrangement worked well, and for the next fifteen years rendezvous were held at various points in the West. Trading was the main business, but there was time for celebration as well. The free trappers, who had spent spring and fall at their work and winter trying to survive, were eager to see old friends and to

Preceding pages: Breech-loading single-shot Sharps rifle; 1855–70; $200–275. Christian Sharps developed the first practical breech-loading rifle in 1848, and his weapons were widely used by plainsmen, particularly buffalo hunters. Leather gun case, Indian made but used by a white trapper; 1870–80; $450–525.

Folk painting in oil; 1870–85; $350–450. Possibly intended to depict the Yosemite area, this painting is typical of many done by artists and amateurs in the West. ▼

Bronze sculpture, *The* ▲ *Frontiersman;* signed by Harry Jackson; dated 1965; $6,000–7,000. From the buckskin leggings to the coonskin cap, this figure accurately portrays the dress of the early western explorers.

Folk painting in oil on canvas; 1890–1910; $250–325. Many ▲ of the so-called western paintings were actually based on European prototypes, hence the unusual combination of alpine architecture and distinctly western trees.

have some fun. Drinking, gambling, and foot and horse racing were the order of the day.

The mountain men were all there. There was Jim Bridger, the noted Indian fighter; Hugh Glass, who had escaped death so many times that his fellows suspected he was just too mean to die (they were wrong—the Blackfeet finally got him); Kit Carson; and, in 1838, a little-known immigrant named John Sutter, who was on his way to California and fame of another sort.

This was a brazen and eccentric lot, given to excesses of every sort. A contemporary chronicler described one of them, Old Bill Williams, an ex-minister, as a man who ''could catch more beaver and kill more horses by hard riding in so doing than any that had ever set trap in the West. He could likewise drink more liquor, spend more money and spend it faster than any other

man. He could also swear harder and longer and coin more queer and awful oaths than any pirate.''

Mountain men could be mean, too, though they had their own peculiar code of honor. One of the meanest was big Mike Fink, who broke the code by not giving his enemy ''an even chance.''

It seems that Fink had had a falling out with a certain fellow named Carpenter, once a close friend. By rendezvous time it appeared that all had been patched up, and the two men began drinking together. This culminated in Fink's betting he could shoot a cup of whiskey off Carpenter's head, a thing he had done before. Only this time, Fink put his bullet between Carpenter's eyes, remarking that it was too bad he had spilled the whiskey.

But the dead man had friends, and one of these,

▲
Sculpture of bears in pewter and glass; by Lucille C. Hampton; 1970; $800–900. The bear was one of the most fearsome animals faced by the mountain men and by the settlers who followed them west. Particularly dreaded was the grizzly of the northern mountains.

Detail of lock and butt of muzzle-loading flintlock
Northwest Bay trade gun; by Barnett; the lock plate is dated
1866; $375–450.
◄

Muzzle-loading rifle with octagonal steel barrel and cherry-wood stock; by Sharps; 1850–60; $450–550. Most mountain men carried rifles of this sort. ▼

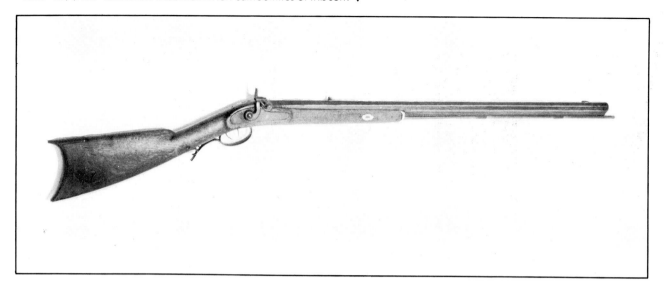

plying Fink with liquor, got him to confess that he had shot to kill. Hearing this, the avenger promptly killed Fink with a pistol bequeathed him by Carpenter.

Despite the many legends it has bred, the era of the mountain men was relatively brief. By 1839 the forests were nearly wrung dry. Like the eastern woods before them, they were almost totally devoid of beaver. At rendezvous the trappers had barely enough to pay for their provisions, and by the following year it was evident that the business was no longer profitable. The supply trains came no more, and the remaining beaver were left to the Indians.

As for the mountain men, their fates varied. A few of them, like Old Bill Williams, became outlaws, the West's first "bad men," preying upon Mexican ranchers and lonely travelers. Others became guides for the wagon trains, which were now beginning to wend their way west; some joined the army; while yet others went down into the plains to try their hands at a new trade—buffalo hunting.

The decline of beaver trapping coincided with the development of the buffalo market. The first explorers had encountered the great, shaggy animals and had seen the Indians hunting them for food and their thick pelts, which could be used for both clothing and shelter. But bison hide was a lot harder to ship to the eastern markets than beaver skin—and there wasn't a great demand for it. Still, by the early 1840s a half-million hides were being harvested annually, most of them destined for use as carriage robes.

Then two things occurred that greatly increased the profitability of the hunt. First, the vast herds of wild Argentine cattle that had previously supplied most of Europe's leather were exhausted through zealous hunting. Merchants searching for a substitute discovered the bison. Second, by the late 1860s, transcontinental rail lines began to snake across the western plains. There was now a market and a means of getting the product to it.

In 1867, when the hunt began in earnest, it must have seemed that the buffalo herds were inexhaustible. At best estimate, nearly 100 million of the great beasts were then roaming the prairies. These were divided into four distinct herds: the Canadian, the Northern, the Central, and the Texan. Of the four, only the Northern had previously been hunted by white men. Yet so effective were the hunters and so terrible their greed that only twelve years later almost all the buffalo were gone, with only a few hundred left to form the nucleus of today's herds.

To understand how this happened one must know something about both the hunted and the hunter. The buffalo were much like cattle, slow-witted and bound by a herd instinct. Marksmen soon found that if approached slowly and from downwind, buffalo would graze quietly while one after another of the herd was shot down. The Indians had known this, but they needed only a few thousand beasts a year, and these they rode down on horseback. The buffalo hunter—or "runner," as he was called—was usually neither Indian nor mountain man. In most cases he was a former railroad worker, soldier, or farmer—despite the

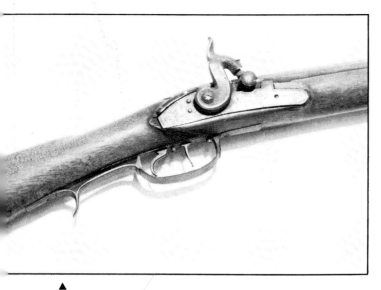

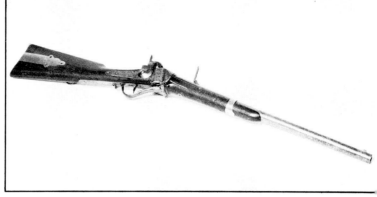

Cap-and-ball carbine; by J. Henry & Son; 1855–65; ▲ $275–350. Large-caliber guns such as this .40-caliber Henry rifle were preferred by buffalo hunters who often had to shoot an animal a dozen times to bring it down.

▲
Detail of breech and stock of rifle; by C. S. Welles, Evansville, Ind.; 1850–65; $550–625. Though they took relatively long to load, these rifles were extremely accurate even at long ranges.

Above: Hunting knife with wrought-iron blade and deer-horn handle; 1850–65; $150–180. Knives such as this were often shaped from old sword or scythe blades. *Below:* Trapper's bait holder in wood; 1900–20; $15–20. ▼

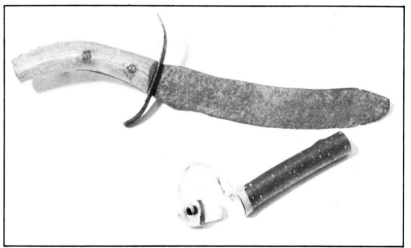

Equipment for cap-and-ball rifle; ▲ 1840–70. *Above:* Lead melting pot; $15–20. *Below:* Ball molds; $28–45. *Center:* Balls and explosive caps. Though they had to buy caps, most woodsmen made their own bullets.

Left: Skinning knife with antelope-horn handle and wrought-iron blade; 1840–50; $175–225. *Right:* Powder horn of cow horn with brass banding and wooden plug; 1860–75; $55–75. ▼

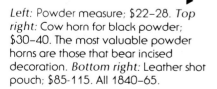

▶
Left: Powder measure; $22–28. *Top right:* Cow horn for black powder; $30–40. The most valuable powder horns are those that bear incised decoration. *Bottom right:* Leather shot pouch; $85–115. All 1840–65.

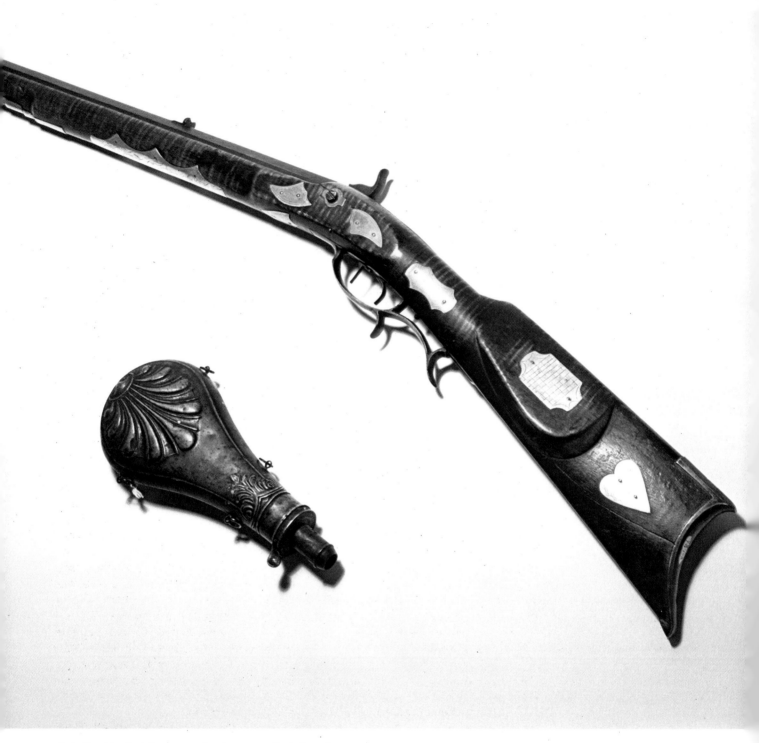

Left: Powder flask in copper; by American Flask Co.; ▲
1870–80; $45–60. *Right:* Pennsylvania half-stock .36-caliber
muzzle-loading percussion rifle; by Joseph Golcher; 1860–65;
$700–850. A known gun-maker's mark enhances the value
of any weapon.

Top: Bowie knife in wrought steel and brass; 1850–60; $1,200–1,500. The Bowie knife, designed by James Bowie, is a legendary weapon of the West. Made to be used in killing bison from horseback, it was known colloquially as the ''Arkansas toothpick,'' and it was a favorite weapon of the plainsman and hunter. The few surviving examples command a high price. *Bottom:* Trade ax in wrought iron; 1840–50; $85–135. ▼

romance associated with theatrical figures like Buffalo Bill Cody, most runners were ordinary men doing a boring but profitable job. It's true that Buffalo Bill killed bison from horseback, but the average hunter didn't. He would just take his heavy-caliber Sharps or Henry rifle and rest it on his knee or a wooden stand and blaze away at the massed herd until it finally spooked. Behind the hunter came his skinners to strip off the hides and the teamsters to haul them to camp where they would be staked out until flint hard and ready for shipment east by rail.

It was a dirty, smelly, but very profitable business. In 1872 there were over two thousand gunners active in western Kansas, taking about fifteen animals each per day. They were getting $2.50 a hide, $2.00 a pound for buffalo hams, $.50 apiece for tongues, and were grinding up the bones for fertilizer. The whole western prairie had become a great slaughterhouse.

These men were killing the buffalo for a living—for others it was a ''sport'' to be indulged in from the windows of trains or from horseback. Most animals killed in this way were left to rot. Even some westerners were shocked by this, as can be seen from the following note taken from an 1872 Topeka, Kansas, newspaper:

> To shoot Buffalo seems a mania. Men come from London, cockneys, fops and nobles, and from all parts of the Republic to enjoy what they call sport. Sport! when no danger is incurred and no skill required. I see no more sport in shooting a buffalo than in shooting an oxe nor so much danger as there is in hunting Texas cattle.

It couldn't last. The excursion hunters and the commercial hunters, the prairie fires and disease, all took their toll. In 1865 the bison dominated the western flatlands; in 1885 the remnants of the herds were curiosities, carefully protected in private sanctuaries.

Despite the romantic legends associated with them, the mountain men and the buffalo hunters left relatively little behind. They were loners and they traveled light. Weapons are the most important relics of their era: the muzzle-loading Kentucky rifles prized by the mountain men and the big .40- to .50-caliber Sharps and Henrys that worked such destruction in the hands of the buffalo runners. There are hand-wrought axes, too, and the knives for fighting or skinning: the Bowie, the famed ''Arkansas toothpick''; and the many Green River blades prized for the quality of their steel.

Clothing is not easily identifiable. Most of the mountain men adopted Indian dress, and the buffalo runners looked pretty much like everyone else working on the plains. Early beaver hats and the military-style headgear affected by some mountain men are much in demand, as are gloves and boots.

Incidental equipment—like the great traps used for bear hunting, the flint and steel to light the evening fire, and the powder horn and bullet pouch—are all collectible. There are also the trophies: the buffalo robes and heads, the deer racks, and the odd steer-horn furniture once so popular in hunting lodges. All these things speak of a time long past, but not forgotten.

Woodsman's hatchet with wrought-iron head; 1830–60; $125–175. Larger and heavier than the traditional fighting axe, this hatchet probably cut down more trees than people. ▼

Buffalo head; 1870–80; $575–650. Early and well-preserved mounted buffalo heads are in great demand for sportsmen's clubs and private collections. ▲

Hat or coat rack in cattle horn; 1900–15; $75–95. Racks like this are the most common of horn collectibles. ▼

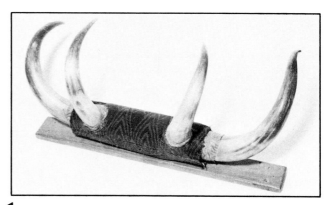

◄ Child's armchair in upholstery over a framework of longhorn-cattle horns; 1880–1900; $750–900. Both amateur and professional hunters gathered a variety of animal horns for use as souvenirs or in rustic furniture such as this piece.

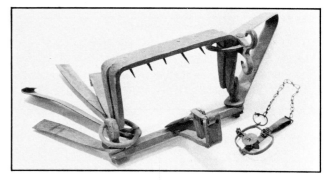

▲ Mounted set of western deerhorns; 1900–20; $65–80. It was only after the extinction of most larger game animals that hunters came to view the deer as a potential trophy rather than just a quick meal.

Left: Bear trap in wrought iron; Montana; 1880–1900; ▲ $225–275. Individually handcrafted for stength and durability, bear traps were a terrible weapon in the trapper's war against his most feared foe. Right: Beaver or small-game trap in iron; 1900–20; $35–45.

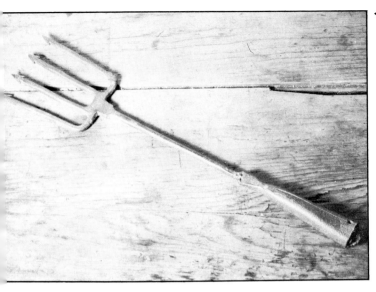

◄ Fish spear in wrought iron; 1870–1900; $55–65. Particularly in spring, fish were an important part of the mountain man's diet. However, it took sharp eyes and good reflexes to spear them.

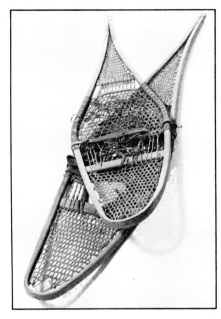

◄ Homemade snowshoes in wood and gut; Colorado; 1900–20; $160–200. Made and used in the Pikes Peak area, these shoes saw many years of hard wear.

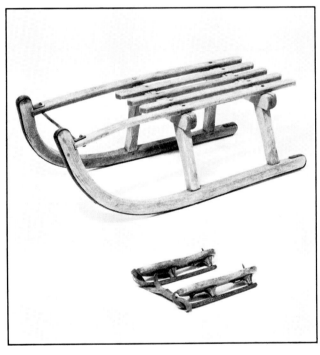

Left: Trapper's pack sleigh in wood with wrought-iron ▲ runners; 1880–1900; $125–160. Pack sleds were usually dragged by hand—horses could not navigate the deep winter drifts. *Right:* Pair of ice skates in wood and iron; 1870–80; $40–55.

Left: Elk-skin pants of the sort worn by mountain men; ▲ 1850–80; $450–550. The beadwork on this pair of pants was probably done by the trapper's squaw. *Right:* Hat in suede; 1870–90; $90–120. This type of hat was worn by both mountain men and Indian scouts.

Back view of mountain man's beaded elk-skin jacket; ▶ Colorado; 1870–90; $850–1,000. Like the Indians among whom they lived, the trappers often showed a fondness for bright clothing.

93

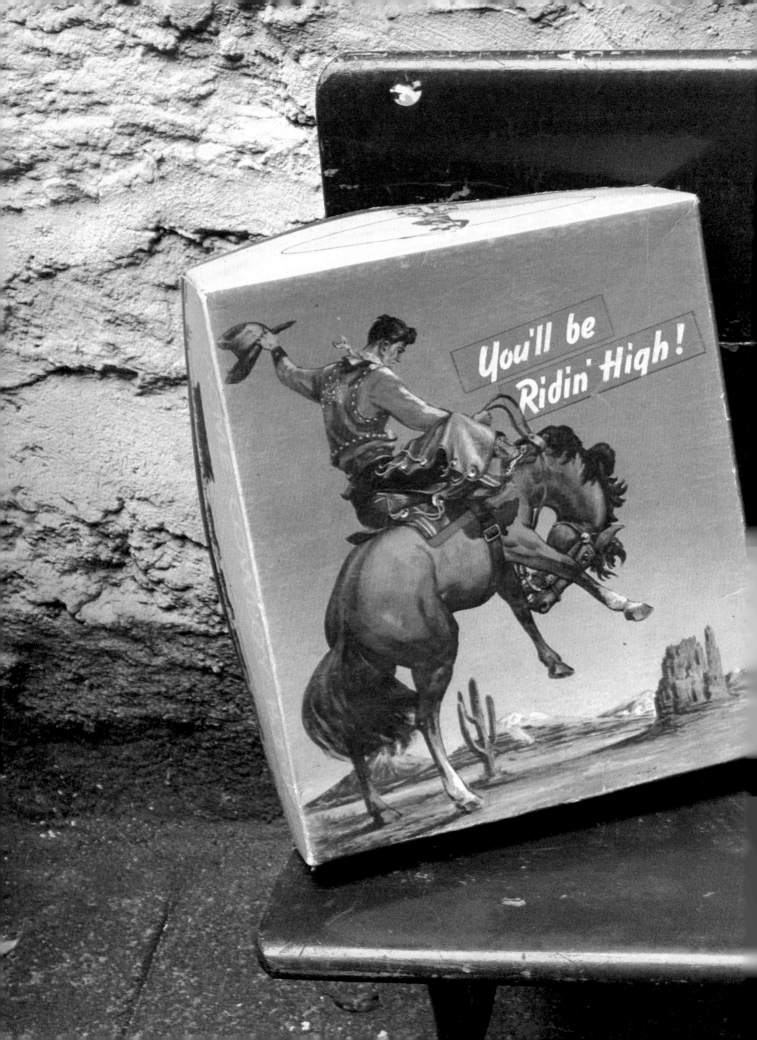

4.

The Cowboys

No individual is more closely associated with the growth of the American West than the cowboy, but the first cowboy wasn't even American. As far back as the eighteenth century, the lonely plains of Argentina and Mexico were patrolled by horsemen, the *vaqueros* (Spanish for "cowmen"), whose job it was to care for the great herds of semiwild cattle that provided South America with beef and Europe with leather.

Herds of similar beasts, descendants of Spanish imports, roamed the arid, cactus and mesquite wastes of Texas's Pecos River country. They were owned, at least nominally, by small ranchers, but they had little value, because Texas was far from eastern markets.

Then came the Civil War, and most of the Texans went off to fight for the Confederacy. With the South blockaded and starving, beef became critical to its cause, and mere boys started leading herds of longhorns east to Louisiana and Georgia. They dodged Union gunboats, swam their beasts across the mighty Mississippi, and earned themselves a name: cowboys.

When the war ended and the men came back, they found that the herds had grown beyond all imagining. The dusty hill country south of San Antonio swarmed with hundreds of thousands of cattle. And a market was developing. In 1865, the Kansas Pacific Railroad reached Abilene in central Kansas. There was a freight yard there and sidings. Beef could be loaded for the eastern markets.

The Texas ranchers had driven cattle before, to the South, to Mexico, and even as far as California across the old Spanish Trail. But none of these journeys compared with what was to come. By 1868, Abilene was a booming cattle town. That year alone over three-hundred thousand longhorns entered its pens. The great drives had begun.

Selling the cattle was one thing—getting them to the railway was another. The Texas longhorn was no milk cow. Descendant of a fighting bull, its wickedly sharp horns spanned eight feet. Fast on its feet and extremely shy, it was far more dangerous than a buffalo. Added to the problematic character of the longhorn was the difficult terrain it had to cross. It was hundreds of miles from the Texas ranches to Kansas, and the way there led through Indian territory, across deserts where there was no water for a hundred miles, and through rough hills where a stampede could result in hundreds of head tumbling to their deaths over cliffs.

Men were needed to guide the cattle to market and care for them on the home ranches. And men came. They were a diverse lot: some were former Confederate cavalrymen; some were the "cowboys" of Civil War fame, now grown to young manhood; and some were "tenderfeet," ex-railroad men or buffalo hunters looking for a way to earn their "dollar a day and grub." All of them had to be tough and resilient to survive the cowboy's hard life.

As a group these men came to be known as cowhands, cowpunchers, or just hands. They adopted, and modified to suit their needs, the Mexican rope, bit, spurs, and saddle. And they set out to do a job.

This task, the cowboy's life, was varied. First there was range work on the ranch where the cattle were born or where they were driven to graze and fatten for market. This work involved a variety of duties and skills. The hand might be a line rider, whose chore was to prevent the feeding cattle from straying onto lands owned by other ranchers and to protect the animals from wolves and rustlers. Once barbed wire appeared in the West, the line rider became a fence rider, with the lonely task of repairing fences smashed by stampeding herds, lightning, or washouts.

Then there were the bog riders, whose tedious and unpleasant duty was extracting cattle from the swamps in which they became mired while trying to find relief from the biting flies that plagued them during the rainy season.

There were also cooks; wranglers, who had the vital task of caring for the ranch horses; foremen, who supervised the whole operation; and a half-dozen other specialties. No matter what task he was assigned, the

Preceding pages: Men's tooled and dyed leather boots with original box; by Acme; 1930–35; $70–85. The brightly decorated box is a bonus to the collector.

cowboy had to be able to ride and to rope. Without these skills he was useless as a hand. Few of the hand's duties were performed on foot, and the rope or lasso was in constant use for everything from roping cattle to dragging in firewood.

At no time were these skills more in evidence than during the roundups. Twice a year, in the spring and in the fall, the ranchers from a given area cooperated in gathering all the cattle roaming the nearby range. Before fences made their appearance, this open land was available to all, and the roundup served to sort out the herds, which had often become mixed while grazing.

The spring roundup was devoted to branding the calves that had been born during the winter. The process required timing and cooperation. Early each morning the hands would be counted off, two by two, to search for cattle. They would then drive the cattle to an assigned assembly area. Once the beasts were gathered, a pair of "ketch hands," usually the best ropers, singled out the new calves, roping them about the neck and hind feet and stretching them immobile on the ground. Then the brander, or "iron man," would apply a red-hot iron bearing the ranch's brand to the calf's flank. At the same time a "knife man" would cut a notch in the critter's ear as further identification. As each calf was marked, a "tally man" would record the act; his book was often the only record an owner had of his herd.

Branding was hot, noisy, and often dangerous work, but it was absolutely essential while thousands of cattle ran together on the same vast acreage.

The purpose of the fall roundup was to sort out mature animals for the market drive. Calves born during the late spring and summer would be branded, of course, but the main goal was to harvest the year's beef.

During the 1880s, fencing, which enabled owners to segregate their herds, put an end to the great roundups, but while they lasted they were one of the most picturesque of western customs.

Following the fall roundup came the year's cattle drive, the cowboy's odyssey and the sine qua non of cattle raising. In Texas, a full-grown steer might bring three to four dollars on the hoof; in Abilene or Dodge City, it was worth fifteen to twenty. The money was there to be made. The only problem was that it was twelve- to fifteen-hundred hard miles from Texas to the railheads, and even farther from the rich Montana grasslands, where some herds were fattened before sale.

There were several routes north that could be

followed. Best known today is the Chisholm Trail named for Jesse Chisholm, a mixed-breed Indian trader who had once followed a path that led south from Abilene to San Antonio. A hundred miles west of Abilene, the so-called Western Trail terminated in the roaring cow town of Dodge City; and even farther on there was the Goodnight-Loving Trail, which followed the Pecos River north to the Colorado Territory.

All these routes had their disadvantages. The Chisholm and the Western passed through lands controlled by the Comanche and the Kiowa, and more than one cowpoke died while defending his herd from Indian attack. The Goodnight-Loving route avoided the hostiles but paid for that with broiling desert, including one stretch nearly a hundred miles long where the animals had to be driven night and day because there were no water holes.

The drives north were hard and dangerous, and only the best hands were allowed to make them, so it became a point of honor among cowboys to have "trailed north." More than one dog-tired sweat-stained cowpoke rode proudly into Abilene or Dodge City, singing one of the many verses that made the "Chisholm Trail" famous:

Come along, boys, and listen to my tale,
I'll tell you of my troubles on the old Chisholm Trail.

We left the ranch on June twenty-third
With a drove of Texas cattle, two thousand in the herd.

I woke up one morning just a riding the trail,
Rope in my hand and cow by the tail.

It's rainin' like hell and gettin' mighty cold,
These longhorn sonsaguns are gettin' hard to hold.

I jumped in the saddle, grabbed holt of the horn,
Best damned cowpuncher ever was borned.

Feet in the stirrups and seat in the saddle,
I hung and rattled with them goddam cattle.

I don't give a damn if they never do stop,
I'll ride as long as an eight-day clock.

With my hand on the horn and my seat in the sky,
I'll quit herding cows in the sweet by and by.

As the verses indicate, the cowboy, or at least his chronicler, was something of a romantic. There is no doubt that most hands adhered to a code that set them apart from most other westerners. They were often shy or taciturn with strangers, a reflection perhaps of the isolation in which they often worked. Among themselves, though, they were warm, friendly, and quick to sing or play a practical joke. As might be expected in a situation where one man's life was often in another's hands, loyalty to the ranch and to other cowpokes was unquestioned.

The average cowhand was unlettered, and because of the isolated, rural conditions under which he habitually worked, he was quite naive about the ways of townsfolk. This made him a ready victim for every cardsharp, barkeep, and floozie working the western cattle towns.

Typically, the hand would collect about a hundred dollars for his three to four months on the trail. It was not uncommon for him to lose it all, in one way or another, within a day or two of hitting a cow town. After all, the town amusements were set up to achieve just that. For example, during the 1870s, Abilene had forty saloons (including the famous Alamo, with a bar so long it was worked by twenty-five bartenders), twenty dancehalls, fourteen gambling dens, and over five-dozen houses of ill repute. Small wonder that cowboys got fleeced and, occasionally, killed.

Although he carried a gun and knew how to use it, the average cowboy was not a professional gunman. He used his weapon to kill wolves or snakes or to put an injured steer out of its misery. Popular legend to the contrary, he rarely drew it against another man, and when he did, he was often gunned down by a more experienced marksman. More than one western bad man fattened his score and his reputation at the expense of cowhands whose courage exceeded their good sense. The traditional ``Cowboys' Lament'' tells it all:

As I passed by Tom Sherman's barroom,
Tom Sherman's barroom quite early one morn,
I spied a young cowboy all dressed in his buckskins,
All dressed in his buckskins, all fit for the grave.

``Once in my saddle I used to go dashing,
``Once in my saddle I used to ride gay;
``But I just took up drinking and then to card playing,
``Got shot by a gambler and dying today.

``Go gather about me a lot of wild cowboys,
``And tell them the story of a comrade's sad fate;
``Warn them quite gently to give up wild roving,
``To give up wild roving before it's too late.''

For many cowboys the warning came too late. They died not only of gunshot wounds, but of disease, accident, and even starvation. Few of them ever got rich. Most of them were loners, with no family ties and few friends outside the bunkhouse, and most lived out their lives owning nothing more than boots, saddle, bedroll, gun, and the clothes on their backs.

The saddle was a particularly important part of the hand's life. Made to order and often costing half-a-year's pay, it was his most valuable possession. When down on his luck, a cowhand would pawn his watch (if he had one) or even his pistol, but never his saddle.

The true era of the cowhand was relatively short. Between 1865 and 1905, he guided 12 million steers and 1 million mustangs from Texas to the railheads. By the latter date fencing and changes in transportation and the economy had made the big drives and the drivers obsolete. There are still men who call themselves cowboys, but they bear little resemblance to their predecessors. (They often oversee their charges from jeeps or even light planes.)

But the old spirit lives on. Wherever cowpunchers gathered there were always horse races, steer wrestling, and other cattle-related contests. On July 4, 1869, a suit of clothing was awarded at one of these meetings. From such festivities has blossomed the professional rodeo circuit, a national institution with hundreds of ropers, wrestlers, and riders, all dedicated to preserving the spirit of the Old West. The extent to which they have succeeded indicates how deeply that spirit is lodged in the American psyche.

The Cowboy in Painting and Sculpture

By the time the cowboy had established himself as a figure on the prairie, the tradition of western painting was well established. Artists like George Catlin (1796–1872), Alfred Jacob Miller (1816–1874), and Peter Rindisbacher (1806–1834) had sketched and painted the native tribes, the trading posts, the mountain men, as well as the picturesque country in which they lived. The pictorial record such men provided is the only visual remnant of those long-gone days.

The role of these early artists was to a great extent documentary. There were no cameras available, so they were often employed on U.S. government expeditions for the specific purpose of recording the people and country that the explorers encountered.

Those who painted and sculpted the cowboy were motivated by a somewhat different ambition. The first of these artists actually lived among the ranch hands, knew them and knew their work. They were drawing their friends and companions. The painters also recognized something that the cowboys seldom perceived—that this period, too, would pass away—and they determined to capture it while they could. As the great painter and sculptor Frederic Remington (1861–1909) noted in a 1905 article for *Collier's* magazine:

> I knew the railroad was coming. I saw men already swarming into the land. I knew the derby hat, the smoking chimneys . . . and the thirty day note were upon us in a restless surge. I knew the wild riders and the vacant land were about to vanish forever. . . . Without knowing exactly how to do it, I began to try to record some facts around me.

Though born wealthy, Remington spent much of his early life wandering the West from Mexico to Canada, working as a cowboy, rancher, and miner. He thus had an intimate knowledge of those whose portraits he created. The same was true of the other great cowboy artist, Charles M. Russell (1864–1926). Russell was a working cowhand for fifteen years, and his art is suffused with a love of the West and its people.

Unfortunately for the average collector, the work of these two artists has become prohibitively expensive. Reproductions and outright fakes of both mens' sculpture abound, making it mandatory that prospective purchasers seek the advice of a reliable expert in the field. Today, most people have to view the works of Russell and Remington in a museum.

Fortunately, a whole new generation of painters and sculptors has risen to follow the great tradition of western art. These men and women do not know the cowboy, but what they lack in firsthand knowledge they compensate for in careful research, training themselves not only as artists, but as historians, in order to make their works constitute an accurate portrayal.

Such living sculptors as Harry Jackson, Lucille Charlotte Hampton, and Frank Polk, and such painters as George Phippen, Barbara Vaupel, and Kenneth Wyatt are representative of a great number of highly competent and creative artists who are bringing the Old West to life on canvas and in stone or bronze. The works shown here are only a portion of the present output, and so great is the attachment of the American artist for the cowboy, that one has no doubt but that the tradition will continue.

Corral gate; northern ▲ Arizona. Corrals and fencing signaled a change in the wide-open expansive West, a change that eventually led to the passing of the traditional cowboy.

Bronze sculpture of two ▶ cowboys roping a steer; by Frank Polk; 1973; $4,500–5,500. This detailed work demonstrates how the animal would be roped around the neck or horns and the hind feet and then pulled to the ground. The procedure required perfect timing and cooperation between cowhands.

Detail of bronze sculpture, *Long Rope and Telescope;* by ▲ Frank A. Polk; 20th century; $3,000–3,750. The hands assigned as range or line riders often had to keep track of widely scattered herds. A telescope was helpful.

Bronze sculpture, *Cold Rain and Slick Rocks;* by K. L. ▲ Mackey; 20th century; $2,500–3,000. The hand's duties often involved rescuing stock, and this was as true for the sheepman as for the cowhand.

Bronze sculpture, *Descent;* by Bob Schrieber; ▲ 20th century; $1,850–2,300. This piece depicts the western saying that ''there ain't a horse that can't be rode, and there ain't a man that can't be throwed.''

◀

Bronze sculpture, *Clayton Danks on Old Steam Boat, Two Champs;* by Harry Jackson; 1977; $10,000–11,000. The bronco buster, whose job was training wild mustangs, was both well paid and highly respected.

Miniature bronze sculpture of western saddle; 20th century; $250–300. Cowboys employed many different types of saddles, depending on locality, personal preference, and the job. ◀

Primitive oil painting of two horses in a storm; late 19th century; $700–850. The horse was the cowboy's constant companion. Without the horse, the job could not be done. ▼

Oil painting, *Changing Pastures*; by Barbara Vaupel; 20th century; $950–1,200. In most areas of the arid West, cattle had to be constantly shifted to prevent overgrazing the range. ▼

Oil painting, *The Roundup;* by George Phippen; 20th century; $900–1,200. The scene depicted is spring roundup and the branding of the new calves.

◀

Oil painting, *The Year It Didn't Rain;* by Kenneth Wyatt; 1979; $850–1,150. Drought was feared by all stockmen. At best it meant a long trek to available water; at worst it could lead to destruction of whole herds.

◀

Oil painting, *Corraling the Cavvy*; by Olaf Wieghorst; 20th century; $800–1,000. The cavvy, or remuda, was the group of horses used by the hands on a particular ranch. They were turned out to winter and in the spring brought back again to the ranch corral. ▼

▲
Oil painting; by George Phippen; 20th century; $900–1,100. Roundups of wild mustangs on the open plains provided the ''horseflesh'' necessary to keep the ranch running. Once the animals were trained, they could be turned loose to graze at night and be rounded up for work in the morning.

Print, *The Little Doggie*; by Gary Niblett; 20th century; $150–175. Keeping track of calves, particularly those that had lost their mothers, could be a full-time job. ▼

Clothing and Equipment

It is indicative of the nature of the cowpuncher's life that his equipment, chiefly horse gear, was considerably more varied and complex than his clothing and personal possessions. Most ranch hands were poor and footloose. They were not married, and their belongings consisted of those items deemed absolutely necessary, such as boots, a bedroll, and whatever else was small enough to be tucked into a saddlebag and thrown across a pony's back.

An idea of what the typical hand looked like can be gleaned from the following description given by a Cheyenne, Wyoming, resident in 1873:

> I observed . . . a drove of ridgy-spined long horn cattle which had been several months eating their way from Texas with their escort of four or five much-spurred horsemen in peaked hats, blue hooded coats, and high boots, heavily armed with revolvers and repeating rifles.

Other common elements of the cowboy's attire were heavy wool or cotton shirts; the traditional bandanna; Levi pants, which were then a novelty; a yellow rain slicker; and, perhaps, a vest.

By far the most important of these items was a good set of boots. Often custom-made, the classic piece of footwear was of soft leather with a high top, sharp toe, thin sole, high heels, and fancy stitchwork. All these features had a purpose (a high heel kept the rider's foot from slipping through the stirrup; the fancy stitchwork stiffened the leather so that the boot top would not curl over and prevented wrinkling at the ankle), and together they created a highly distinctive shoe. Pre-1900 boots are hard to come by today and are expensive.

Hats, too, were considered a necessity. Though they varied from region to region (brims were wider in the hot Southwest), hats had a basic form that set them apart from the headgear worn by noncowpokes: wide sunshade brim; high, insulating crown; gray or brown color.

Some cowhands sported fancy belt buckles, but most did not, and the so-called western buckle is for the most part a creation of the rodeo rider and the movie lot. A cowboy was far more concerned with his chaps, or chaparreras, leather overalls that protected him from the thorny bushes common in parts of the Southwest. Chaps, too, are highly collectible today.

The saddle was the cowboy's most important possession, so vital that it was common to say of a deceased puncher that he had "sacked his saddle." Like boots, saddles were often custom-made, costing as much as a full year's salary. Individual needs and specific circumstances led to the development of various saddle types, including the Brazos; the Nelson; and the Ellenburg (the Stetson of saddles), which eventually became the rodeo association contest saddle.

Spurs, or "gut hooks," as they were sometimes called, were produced in great variety. Large-roweled spurs were preferred because they had more points and were therefore not likely to dig into a horse's flank. Among collectors, decorated spurs or those inset with silver in the Mexican manner are particularly prized.

Bits and bridles form another interesting area of collectibles. The bridle, or "headstall," is the horse's headgear and the foundation upon which the bit and reins are anchored. Bits are usually made of iron and steel and come in three variations: the snaffle, the bar, and the curb. Like the spur, the cowboy used the bit to suggest pain—and thereby produce a given reaction—not to cause pain. Cowboys were rarely cruel to their horses.

Bridles, bits, and reins are all collected today, with older, unusual forms and those that have been embellished with metalwork or fancy leather regarded as most desirable.

Another piece of collectible equipment is the wrought-iron branding iron, which was used to burn a ranch mark on calves. During the heyday of the open range, there were over a thousand different ranch brands in use as well as various "county" brands and "road" brands used on herds of cattle being driven north to market. As a result, branding irons are so common today that they are being made into such unlikely objects as candleholders!

Other objects of interest to the collector are the various implements found in the ranch chuck wagon, the ropes used in roping horses and cattle, stirrups, and hackamores. Those who are interested in rodeo history seek out such paraphernalia as the ropes and bells used in bull-riding and bronc-riding saddles.

Black Mexican-style sombrero; Texas; 1900–10; ▶
$145–190. The sombrero was adopted by the
early ranch hands and modified to suit their
purposes. It was most popular in border regions.

▲
Decorated belt buckle in brass on German silver;
made in Nevada; 1930–40; $25–30. Though
called ''cowboy'' belts, most such belt buckles
were never used by working cowboys.

Light-tan cowboy hat in the form popularized by ▶
Tom Mix movies; 1920–30; $125–175. Hats
served many purposes: as sunshades, umbrellas,
drinking cups, and even signal devices.

Light-gray cowboy hat; 1940–50; $75–100. ▶
Though not very old, this hat was used on the
range and shows signs of wear. Most cowboys
were so fond of their headgear that they wore it
until it fell apart.

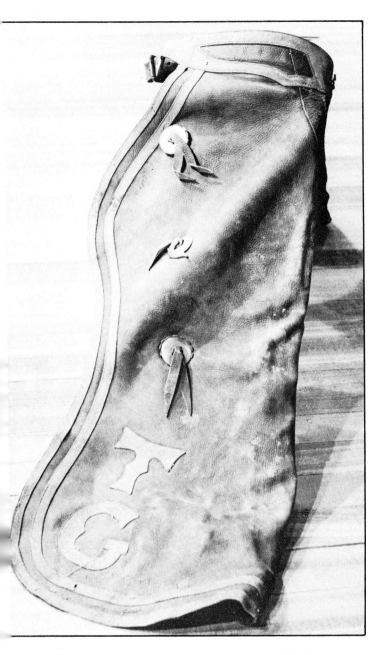

Pair of chaps in black angora wool; 1890–1900; $400–500. Called "hair pants," chaps of this sort were used on the northern plains. When wet they became soggy and uncomfortable and took on a strong odor. Hard to find today, they are much prized by collectors. ▼

Pair of "bat-wing"-style chaps in leather; 1930–40; ▲ $200–275. Bat-wing chaps have been popular with cowhands for a long time because, unlike earlier types, they snap on and do not require one to pull off his spurs to shed them.

Chaps in leather with ranch brand in metal studs; 1910–20; ▶
$275–350. Chaps served as protection and, contrary to
popular opinion, they were not worn when working on foot
or on visits to town.

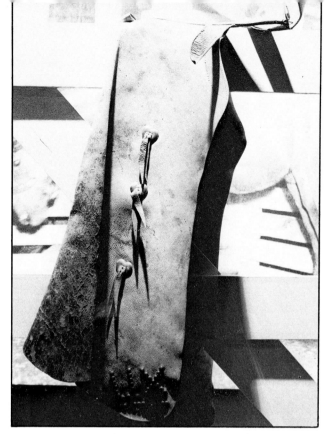

Boots in leather; 1915–25; $180–270 the pair. ▼

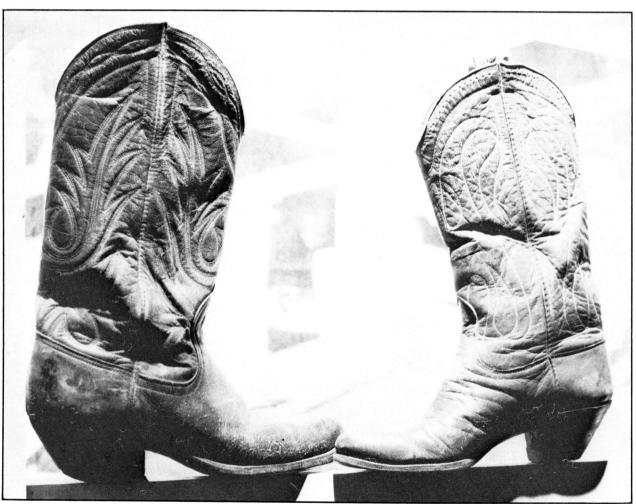

Boot in decorated leather; 1930–40; $200–260 the pair. ▶
Fancy boots like this were more likely to be worn in town
than on the range. Note the sharp toe, designed to facilitate
picking up the near stirrup on a wheeling or prancing horse.

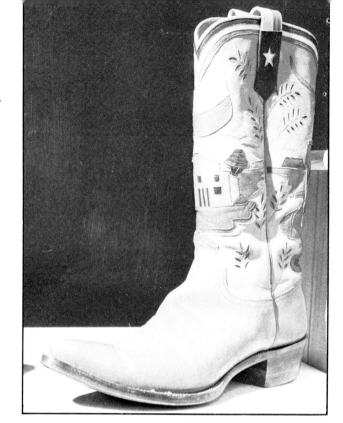

Boots in tan leather; 1930–40. *Left:* Woman's
''peewee''-style short boot; $90–130. Cowmen never
favored the short boot, for it picked up too much gravel.
Right: Man's high boot; $125–175. ▼

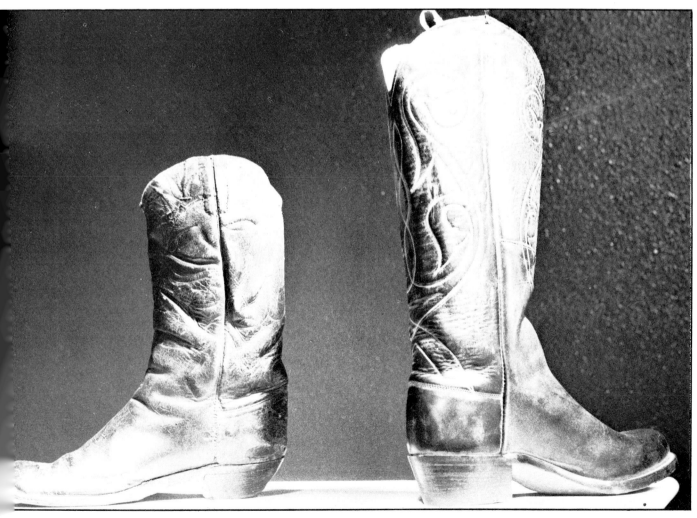

Cowboy accessories in ▲ leather; 1870–90. *Left:* Saddlebag; $155–205. *Right:* Leather-covered glass drinking canteen; $90–130. The canteen was a vital part of any western horseman's equipment.

McClellan-type army ▶ saddle in leather; by Butler Co.; 1870–80; $325–400. Cowboys who could not afford custom saddles could use old army ones, but such saddles were not well-suited to range work.

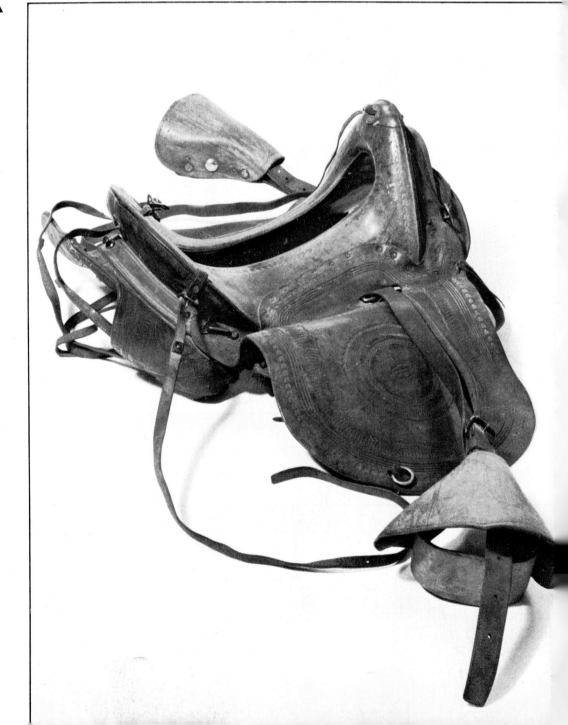

Stock saddle; 1880-90; $475-575. Note the high horn used in roping and the wooden stirrups known variously as ''ox yokes'' or ''dog-house'' stirrups. ◄

Military saddle in brass and leather over iron; 1875-85; $200-275. This type of saddle was widely used in the West. ▼

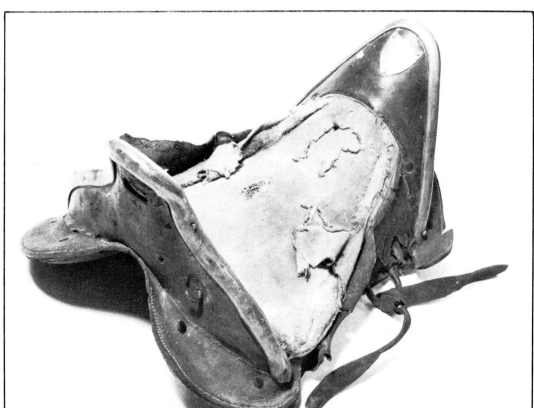

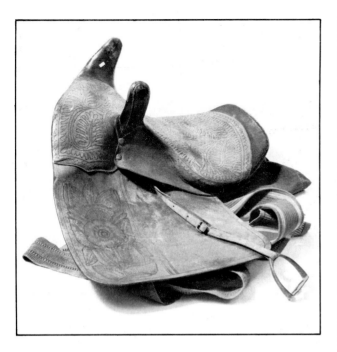

Woman's sidesaddle with elaborate tooled decoration; ▲ Jacob's Patent; 1890; $250–350. Though many women used them, sidesaddles were neither comfortable nor particularly practical.

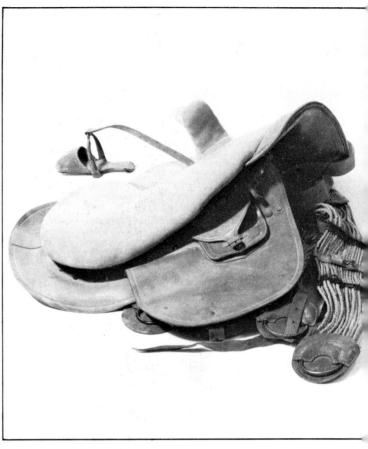

Woman's sidesaddle with cinch and unusual slipper-type ▲ stirrup; 1900–10; $200–275. Note the interesting padded saddle surface.

Bareback saddle in leather; 1920–25; $160–220. Once rodeo riding became a popular western activity, a variety of specialized saddles was developed for the various events. ▼

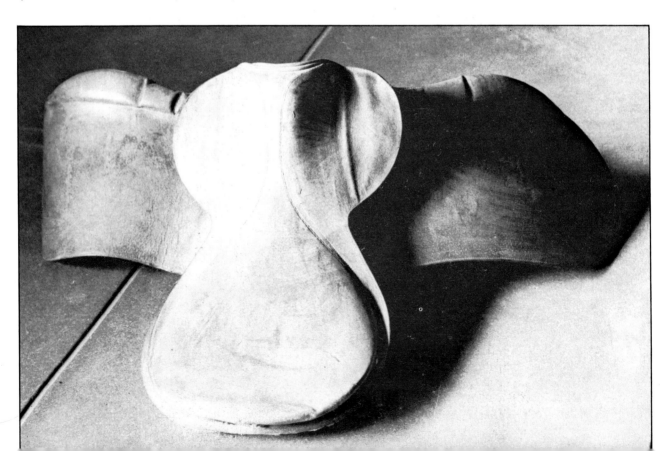

Bareback saddle with cinch and rigging; 1940–50; $175–250. Like all rodeo events, bareback riding requires skill and stamina.
◄

113

English-style saddle in decorated leather; 1935–45; $235–285. Though frowned upon by the cowboy, the English saddle was frequently used in the West, primarily by well-to-do horse owners. ▼

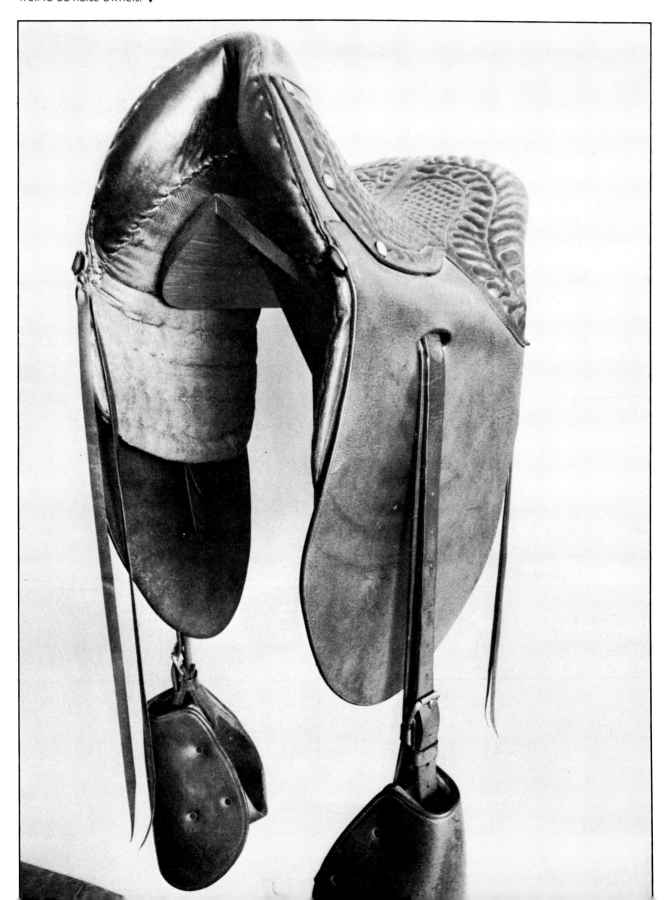

Specialized saddle used by steer wrestlers; 1950–55;
$200–250. Rodeo is in a very real sense the successor to the
life of the cowboy. The wandering from competition to
competition, the danger, and the small financial return for
most riders are things the old-time cowpoke would well
understand. ▼

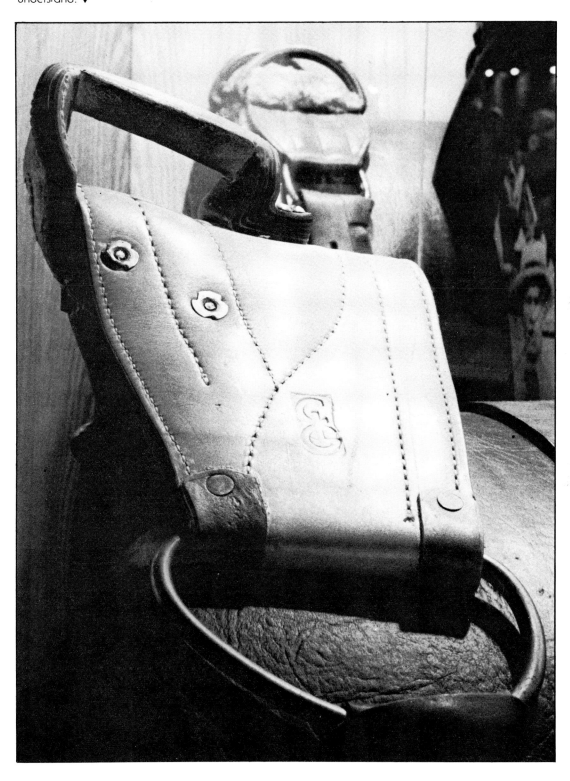

Spurs in steel and leather; New ▲
Mexico; late 19th century;
$125–175. Though they looked
formidable and were called such
things as "gut hooks" and "can
openers," spurs were intended to
instruct, not to injure.

Pair of so-called humanitarian ▶
spurs; 1900–20; $75–90. This
type of spur was preferred by the
U.S. Army.

116

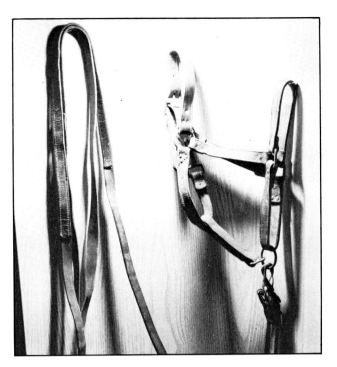

Reins and halter in leather; 1900–10; $90–135. Reins used by cowboys were usually of leather, though they were also made of rawhide or even horsehair. The bridle and halter went around the horse's head.
◀

Bareback rider's bridle with characteristic, thick single rope rein; 1920–30; $75–100. ▼

Variation of the bar bit in cast iron; 1900–10; $30–40. There ▶ are three basic types of bit; bar, curb, and snaffle. All were widely used in the West. In each case, the purpose served was controlling and directing the horse.

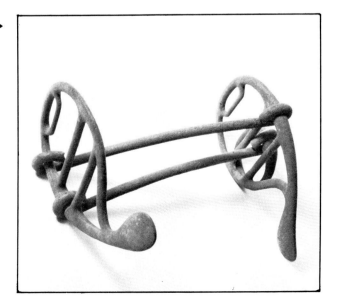

Rodeo flank strap; 1940–50; $90–120. ▶
Bound around the underbody of a horse
or bull, the strap's strange feel makes
the animal buck higher.

▲
Rope and bell used in rodeo bull riding; 1950–60; $60–75. Bull riding is one of the most dangerous rodeo activities.

◄
Detail of cowboy's rope; 1890 1900; $175 250. Nicknamed ''string,'' ''whale line,'' or even ''cat gut,'' the rope was an essential tool of the cowhand. It was usually made of manila, though rawhide and maguey (fiber of the century plant) were also used.

Various types of ▲
horseshoes; 1880–1900;
$3–5 each. A traditional
symbol of luck, the old
horseshoe has been
collected for generations.
Specialists distinguish
between types and
between those used for
younger or older steeds.

Hobbles in cast iron;   ▶
1870–90; $70–80. Hobbles
were used to control horses
turned out to pasture. They
allowed horses to graze,
but made it more difficult
for Indians or rustlers to
drive them off.

▲
Detail of branding iron in wrought iron; 1870–85; $110–140. Branding was designed to enable owners to distinguish among the cattle running on an open range.

Group of branding irons in wrought and cast iron; 1890–1910; $15–35 each. During the height of the cattle drives, there were over a thousand different brands in use in the West, most in some way related to the name of a ranch or ranch owner.
◄

The Cowboy's Amusements

Ranch hands' amusements were few—music, jokes, and tall tales on the trail; hard drinking, women, and gambling in town—and with their work load, they didn't have much time for any of it. But they did what they could.

Drinking was probably the thing most men looked forward to after coming in off a cattle trail so thick with dust that "a buzzard would have to wear goggles and fly backward to keep from choking to death in it." With rotgut rye a quarter a shot and beer almost for the asking, it didn't take a trail-weary hand long to get loosened up. In the words of the old tippling song "Rye Whiskey":

If the ocean was whiskey and I was a duck,
I'd dive to the bottom and never come up.
But the ocean ain't whiskey and I ain't no duck,
So we'll round up the cattle, and then all get drunk.

Saloons jammed the streets of every cow town, and the whiskey bottles and stoneware jugs that their proprietors threw out the back door are still being dug up by western collectors.

With a few stiff drinks in him, the cowhand's thoughts might turn to gambling, to "makin' his pile" so that he could get that spread or new saddle he'd had an eye on. The town could satisfy this urge, too, with faro rooms and gambling halls to suit every taste. Naturally, most of the games were rigged. Professional cardsharps used shaved decks and elaborate mechanical devices to cheat their opponents, and not being "town wise," cowpokes were among the most gullible.

If the cowpunchers did catch on to the chicanery, it could get messy. Cowboys were clannish, and a gunfight with one could involve the whole ranch, like that night in Newton, Kansas, in 1871, when a grudge fight in Tuttle's Place left nine men dead in less than five minutes.

It would be unfair and inaccurate to picture the range rider as a violent man. He might shoot up the town lights and get thrown in the hoosegow for his trouble, but for the most part he took his pleasure without bloodshed.

After all, he took his work and turned it into play—the rodeo, which has been a major part of western life for nearly a century. Even without the formal contests, cowboys were always quick to try a little roping, quarter-horse racing, or marksmanship.

Cowboys also had their music. The great number of songs that have come out of the West are a clear testimonial to the ranch hands' love of song. Every bunkhouse had a fiddle, guitar, and banjo, and if these instruments were too frail to survive life in the saddle, there was always the sweet potato or the harmonica to tuck into pocket or saddlebag.

Over the past decade collectors have been scouring the pawnshops and second-hand stores of the western states, looking for musical instruments used by the cowboys. There are still quite a few examples of these around, but they are beginning to get expensive.

Most cowpunchers smoked. The tobacco-pouch string dangling from a breast pocket has become a hallmark of the western male. Lacking contemporary knowledge of the deleterious effects of tobacco, the cowboy smoked and chewed just about anything he could get his hands on, leaving behind in the process a raft of collectible cigar boxes, tobacco cans, and cigarette packs.

There were other leisure-time activities. Some men whittled. A few did decorative leather work or made lariats, but the cowboys lacked the time to produce the folk art achieved by men who led more sedentary lives. Rather than objects, the cowhand left behind his songs, his vision, and his land.

Gaming wheel; Colorado; early 20th century; $200–275. Made from a wagon wheel, this device is typical of those used to fleece cowboys in the rough towns at the end of the long Texas-Kansas trail.

◀

Gambler's "hold out"; ▶ 1900–10; $1,850–2,100. Though now rare, devices like this were once in frequent use in the gambling halls of the Old West. The sharpster would conceal the rig under his vest, and pressure on the spring device concealed behind his knee would cause a desired card to fall into his hand.

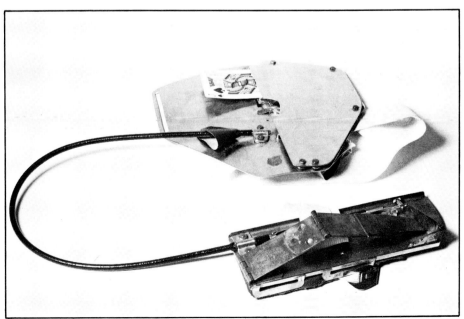

Stoneware whiskey jug; by Western Pottery Co., Denver, ▶
Colo.; 1905–15; $65–75. Whiskey was transported and sold
in heavy stoneware jugs. This one is unusual in that it was
made in the West, where there were few potteries. Most
such receptacles came from east of the Mississippi.

Left: ``Case'' gin bottle; 1890–1900; $20–30. *Right:* Rye
bottle; 1870–80; $20–25. Old green-glass bottles like these
are found in abundance around the cow towns of the West.▼

Guitar in wood inlaid with mother-of-pearl; 1900–10; $145–195. The guitar was the cowboy's favorite instrument, even though its fragility made it an unlikely trail companion (unless carried in the cook's wagon). ▼

Fiddle in dark wood inlaid with light; 1880–90; $165–225. The so-called coffin case ▲ accompanying this fiddle is, itself, a popular collectible.

Accordian in wood and
leather inlaid with
mother-of-pearl;
1890–1910; $175–250.
The ''squeeze box'' was
a lot more rugged than
it looked and was often
taken on the long trail
to provide music
around the campfire. ▶

Banjo in wood and hide with steel fittings; ▶
1870–80; $200–250. Western instruments this
old are seldom seen. The banjo was
a popular bunkroom musicmaker.

126

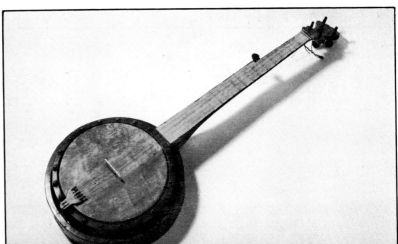

▲
Ukulele in wood inlaid with
mother-of-pearl; 1910–20;
$110–150. Though it arrived
on the scene rather late, the
ukulele was popular with
20th-century cowhands,
perhaps in part because of its
use by silent-film cowboys.

◄

Detail of elaborate
mother-of-pearl inlay in the
form of an eagle set in
ukulele; 1900–10; $250–325.
Decorative work of this quality
raises an instrument to the
level of folk art.

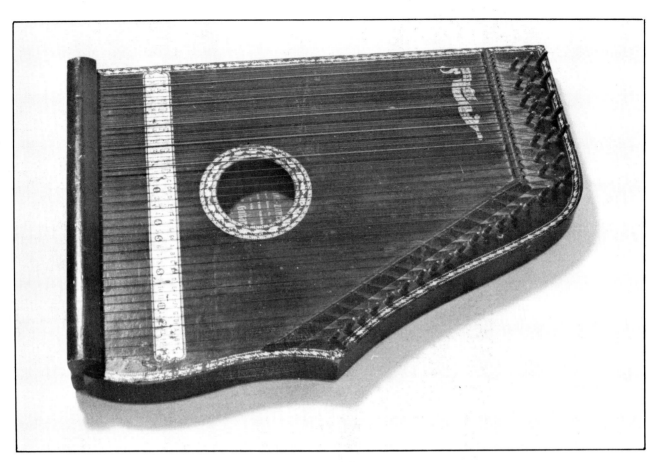

Zither in wood with inlaid mother-of-pearl decoration; ▲ patented 1894; $115–155. Though primarily a woman's instrument, the zither was often seen at ranch hoedowns and musicals.

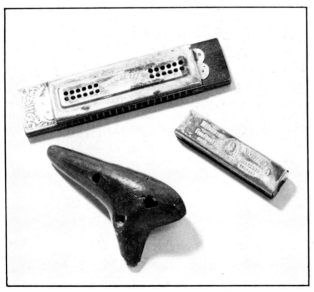

▲
Chewing tobacco box in lithographed tin; 1900–15; $30–40. Most cowhands chewed cut plug. It was easier to handle (and, in dry brush, safer) than rolling tobacco. Some hands got so proficient at spitting tobacco juice that they claimed they could blind a rattlesnake at ten paces!

◄ *Top:* Mouth organ, or harmonica; Hohner's Best; 1890–1900; $90–110. *Left:* Sweet potato, or ocarina, in clay; 1880–1900; $60–75. *Right:* Harmonica; Hohner's Newest Best; 1910–20; $45–55. Harmonicas and ocarinas, simple to play and easy to carry, were the most common cowhand musical instruments.

Cigar boxes in lithographed ▲ paper on wood; 1910–30; $18–38 each. The cigar was a sign of status pretty much confined to the foreman or ranch owner—or, perhaps, a cowpuncher feeling his oats after a few stiff drinks.

◄

Novelty match holder in cast iron; 1890–1900; $25–35. The sort frequently found in cow-town bars and gambling houses.

129

Saddle in leather decorated with brass tacks; Colorado; 1870–90; $225–300. The traditional cowboy saddle was derived from earlier Spanish forms and was designed to facilitate cattle roping in difficult country. ◀

Polychromed bronze sculpture of ▶ a cowboy, *Where the Trail Forks;* by Harry Jackson; 1962; $7,000–8,000.

Enamelware coffeepot, plate, ▶ and cup, and knife and fork in steel with wood handles; all 1890–1920. Coffeepot; $25–35. Plate; $10–14. Cup; $4–6. Knife and fork; $13–17 the pair. Sturdy and rustproof, enamelware was used extensively in the cowboy chuck wagon.

WHERE THE TRAIL FORKS
HARRY JACKSON

Guns of the American Cowhand

A wide variety of handguns and rifles was used in the West, and all are considered collectors' items. Most cowboys weren't gunfighters. Indeed, a reputation for an itchy trigger finger was a sure way to lose a trail job. There were enough problems on the range without having to contend with homegrown shoot-outs. Still, the cowpuncher usually packed a weapon. It was expected of him, and it could be a necessity on the trail, where anything from a loco steer to a cattle rustler might show up.

There is no doubt that the average ranch hand would spend more of his hard-earned cash on a saddle or a pair of boots than on a pistol or rifle. Many men employed surplus military guns, such as the Remington army model .36- and .44-caliber percussion-type revolvers.

Remington was one of the great names in western handguns. Smith & Wesson, which developed the first metallic cartridge revolver in the 1860s, also had a share of the market (Buffalo Bill Cody carried an S&W .44-caliber American), but the leading manufacturer was Colt.

Samuel Colt, perhaps the most famous of all American gun makers, had been dead for ten years when his firm patented the Model 1872 Colt revolver, a six-shot .45-caliber single-action weapon. Known as the Frontier Model or, later, as the Peacemaker, the Colt .45 brought little peace to the West. Relatively inexpensive, rugged, and effective up to a range of one hundred yards, the Model '72 became the favored weapon of the western outdoorsman, be he cowboy, farmer, or gunman.

The arrival of the Colt .45 coincided with the highly romanticized era of the gunfighter and the "fast draw." Though the tales of individual gun duels and sharpshooting exploits have been greatly exaggerated (most gunmen shot from ambush, and it took the Earp brothers nearly forty shots to kill three men at close range at the O.K. Corral), there is no doubt that professional gunslingers spent long hours perfecting their quick draw and devised clever ways of carrying their pistols to facilitate that movement. Cowboys could seldom afford the quarter a cartridge it cost to practice, and the low-slung open holsters favored by the killers would have soon led to a lost weapon on the trail.

Still, nearly everyone had his Colt, Remington, or Smith & Wesson. In fact, the custom of gun toting was so prevalent that one Texan of the period remarked that "I would as soon go out into the street without my pants as without my Colt." The big names in gunfighting (men who were being immortalized by western writers like Ned Buntline) vied in their (paid) endorsements of specific handguns. Wild Bill Hickok, Pat Garrett, and Bat Masterson all carried Peacemakers, while Cody swore by his Smith & Wesson, and the ill-fated Custer owned a Remington .44.

For practical purposes, rifles were of more use to the cowhand than pistols. They were more accurate, particularly at long range, and more powerful, important matters in sport hunting or in fighting off renegade Apache. Since they were shorter and easier to carry and handle on horseback, carbines were preferred. Again, military weapons like the .50-caliber Spencer and the rolling-block Remington .44 were the initial choice.

The all-time favorite and the gun that is said to have "won the West" is the Winchester .44–.40, an 1873 model twelve- or fifteen-shot repeating rifle. Sturdy but lightweight, extremely accurate, and packing a real wallop, the Winchester was a terror to the Plains Indians. When it was redesigned in 1878 to take the same size cartridge as the Colt Peacemaker, the two weapons swept the western market.

Gun collecting is a major American hobby, with dozens of books on the subject, several popular magazines, and a following that numbers in the hundreds of thousands. No collection of cowboy memorabilia would be complete without a rifle and a pistol, just as no cowhand would have headed down the trail without such company.

Single-action .45-caliber Peacemakers; by Colt; 1875–85. *Above:* Bisley Model with extended handle; $850–1,000. *Below:* Standard Model; $1,000–1,200. ▼

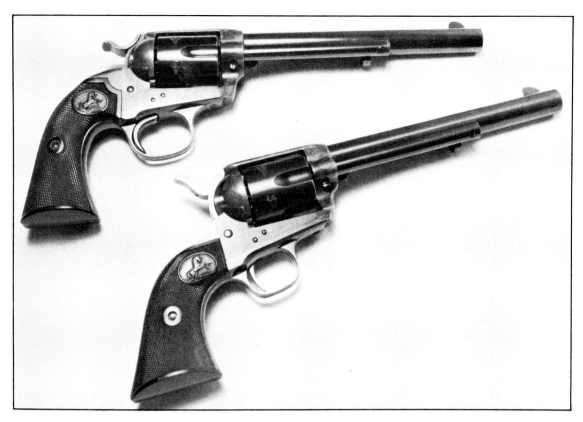

Short-barreled single-action Peacemaker with mother-of-pearl handle and engraved ▲ decoration; by Colt; 1873–80; $7,500–8,000. Custom-made presentation models are highly prized by collectors.

Tooled and dyed calfskin cowboy boots in adult and child sizes; 1930–40; $60–85 the pair. More than mere footwear, the cowboy boot, in the hands of a skilled bootmaker, becomes a work of art. ▼

Men's western, or cowboy-style, twill riding pants and dress shirt; both 1940–50. Shirt; $35–40. Pants; $90–120. The western range rider has never been conservative in his dress clothes, and bright colors are customary, particularly in shirts. ◀

Gaucho-type women's western riding hat in suede; 1930–40; $70–90. Hats, like boots, are among the most popular collectibles from the West. ▼

Yoke-front cowboy dress shirt; 1930–40; $45–55. The double thickness of material at the shoulder was intended to protect the wearer's shoulders from the western sun. ▶

◀
Left: Western-style riding boots in suede; 1945–55; $75–90 the pair. Note the unusually narrow toe. *Right:* Women's western riding pants in cotton; 1940–50; $90–120.

.44-caliber New Model #3 six-shooter; by Smith & Wesson; 1875–90; $400–475. Buffalo Bill Cody packed an ``S&W,'' and these efficient and relatively inexpensive revolvers were carried by many cowhands. ▼

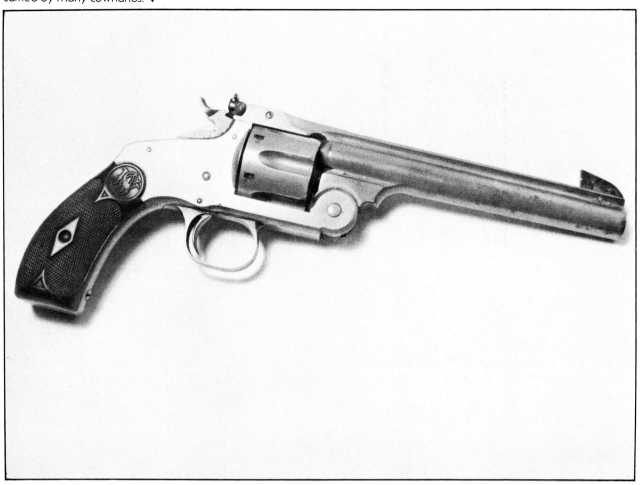

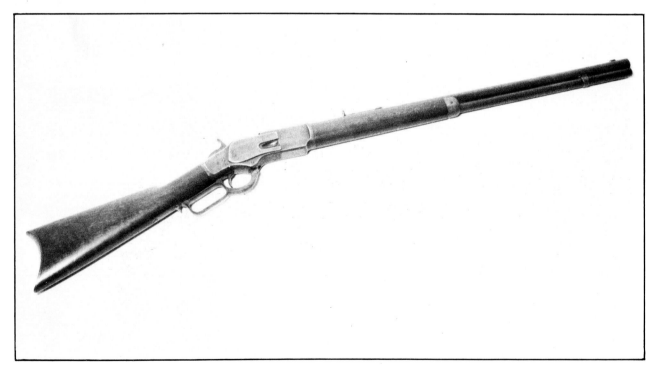

Model 1873 .44-.40-caliber repeating rifle; by Winchester; $550–600. ▲
The Winchester was inexpensive and reliable, and ranch hands could not afford to be without one.

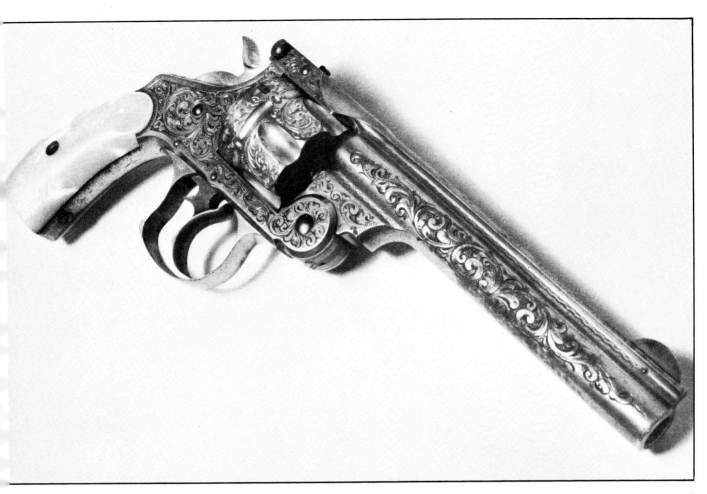

Presentation Model ▲
double-action revolver; by
Smith & Wesson; 1875–90;
$5,000–6,000. Beautifully
tooled engraving, pearl
handle, and gold and
silver plate enhance a
common weapon.

Philadelphia Derringer in
engraved steel and wood;
by Derringer Co.; 1865–75;
$750–850. Few cowboys
carried these nasty little
.44-caliber weapons. They
were of little use against
rattlesnakes or rustlers,
having but a single
purpose—to kill people at
close range. ▶

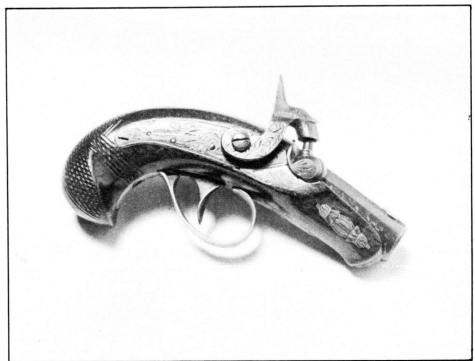

5.

Days of Forty-nine

Bottle collecting is one of America's great pastimes, and one of the bottles most popular with collectors is a pale-blue flask bearing an embossed representation of a prospector, pack on back, stick in hand, and face set to the West. Inscribed above his head, the words "FOR PIKE'S PEAK" symbolize the lust for precious metals that, after the California gold strike of 1848, emptied towns and sent whole generations streaming into the ore-rich mountains.

Nothing is more closely associated with the West than the legends of mineral wealth and the forty-niners who set out to find it. However, these Anglo argonauts were not the first gold seekers in the West, for as early as 1536 wandering Spanish adventurers had brought back tales of the seven golden cities of Cibola. The cities, alas, proved to be made of rock and mud, and it was over three hundred years later that another Spaniard, Francisco Lopez, found gold-bearing sand in a small stream near what is now Los Angeles. Some panning was done during 1842, but nothing much came of it, and the matter was soon forgotten.

Not so with the next find. The year was 1848 and the site Sutter's Mill in northern California. John Sutter, a Swiss immigrant, had established a farm, fort, and trading post in the fertile Sacramento Valley during the 1830s. As his interests expanded, he found himself in need of timber and sent his foreman, James Marshall, to establish a sawmill on the banks of the American River close to the wooded slopes of the Sierra Nevada.

While digging a tailrace for the mill, Marshall spotted flakes of gold—"color," as it came to be known—in the streambed. He brought the material to Sutter. It was gold. They tried to keep the find a secret, but someone talked. The story was to prove a familiar one in the West during the next sixty years.

The find was made in January. In March a drunken prospector appeared on the streets of San Francisco. In his hand was a bottle, and in the bottle were gold nuggets. His cry, "Gold! Gold on the American River!" rang through the streets of the sleepy port. Within days

San Francisco and nearby Monterey became ghost towns as all who could walk or ride poured into the nearby hills. Ships lost their crews, troops deserted, and stores stood empty as the human tide crashed against the Sierra.

These first prospectors were for the most part neither well equipped nor quite sure of what they were after. They scooped up gold-bearing sand in washtubs and pie plates and scratched it out of crevasses with Bowie knives. A few struck it rich, but most soon tired of their unprofitable sport. Of course, there were experienced men, and some of them seemed to enjoy practical jokes, "whizzers," they called them, almost as much as they liked finding a good claim.

For example, in 1850 gold was discovered on the rugged north fork of California's Yuba River. One of the first prospectors in was Pike Sellers, a Missouri man and a great wag. Sellers had been working the stream for several days and doing well at it when he spotted a Johnny-come-lately heading for his claim. Pike didn't need competition, but he did need a good laugh, so, quick as a flash, he grabbed a handful of nuggets and ran for the nearest pine tree. When the greenhorn reached him, the old prospector was hacking away at the bark like a crazed beaver.

"What you be doing?" cried the interloper.

"Why, what you think, you tarned fool," replied Pike. "I'm a seeking gold." And just then he pulled a big nugget out from under the bark. Just to put the icing on the cake, Sellers explained that the higher up the tree, the larger the nuggets found.

It didn't take much encouragement to get the newcomer way up the nearest pine, and, with that, yet another whizzer was born.

Most prospectors were less naive, and they soon decided that if there was gold in California there should be some in the surrounding states as well. In the 1850s and 1860s strikes were made in Arizona, Nevada, and Colorado. The names of these mother lodes and the cities that grew up about them are the stuff of legends.

Preceding pages: Ore cars in iron and steel; Edger Mine, Colo.; ca. 1930; $300–400 each. Such vehicles were used to transport ore from the mine to the smelting facilities.

There is Central City in Colorado, where the famous newspaperman Horace Greeley found over four thousand people living in tents and the very ground beneath his feet full of gold. (It should have been, for his publicity-conscious hosts had "salted" the area by firing shotgun charges of gold dust into it!)

Between 1859 and 1875, Central City produced over $65 million in gold, but it was hardly the richest strike. The mines at Tombstone, Arizona, turned out close to $80 million in sixty years, and the famous Homestake Mine in South Dakota's Black Hills is still going strong with over $.5 billion logged so far.

Nor was gold the only thing found in the western hills. In 1859, a rich vein of silver sulfide was discovered on Nevada's Carson River. Called the Comstock Lode after one of its finders (he sold out his share for less than $12,000), this claim was worked for $300 million in two decades.

Then there was the Hidden Treasure Mine in Nevada's barren White Mountains, said to be so rich that $75,000 in silver was realized just by running the walls of a prospector's stone house through the mill. True or not, such tales had an instant effect on prospectors. By 1870, over thirteen thousand claims had been filed in the White Mountains alone.

In loss of human life and sheer misery, the price paid for this wealth was very high. More than one prospector was killed before he could reach town to register his claim, and even registration was no guarantee of ownership. At Gold Hill, Nevada, claims were "recorded" in a loose-leaf folder kept under the bar in a local saloon. With record keeping like that, small wonder that men lost their lives and lawyers got rich disputing claims.

There were always those who would not pan or dig for their gold. Outlaws roamed the hills and mining camps, watching for miners with a "poke" of gold dust. Nor were the Indians inactive. In Arizona, over four hundred men died during the 1860s and 1870s, victims of the Apache, who regularly raided wagon trains carrying bullion to Phoenix from the rich Vulture Mine at Wickenburg.

But there were other, safer ways of fleecing the miner. Most claims were located in desolate areas, far from established communities. So the towns went to the mines, springing up overnight on mountainsides and in the desert. This meant that everything cost more, and the miner paid. In San Francisco, by the summer of '49, eggs were selling for a dollar each, and the only bathtub in Tonopah, Nevada, was rented out. The tub was filled only once, and customers paid according to how many times the water had been used. A sign outside the bathroom proclaimed, "First Chance, $1; second chance, 50¢; all others 25¢."

Merchants rushed to the new settlements, and more than one got rich by "grub staking" a prospector down on his luck. In Oro City, Colorado, a storekeeper named Tabor gave two German miners seventeen dollars worth of supplies and ended up with a share in the Little Pittsburgh Mine, which he was able to sell the next year for a half million dollars!

But Tabor was little better than the men he fleeced. He made money hand over fist for a decade, married the legendary "Baby Doe" (whose favorite occupation was buying horses and coaches to match her Paris gowns), and went broke, ending up where he had started, as a postmaster.

There were shrewder men who made and kept millions. One of these was Marcus Daly, first of the Montana "Copper Kings." Daly started out prospecting outside Butte, Montana. By the 1880s, his smelters dominated the Butte landscape, laying down a blanket of sulfur fumes so thick that trees died and streetlights had to be kept burning during the day. When finally convinced that his industry wasn't all that healthy for residents, Daly relocated the smelters in a valley some twenty miles west of Butte, where he is said to have laid out the main road by instructing his foreman to "run it north and south through that nearest cow."

Daly's attitude toward people and, particularly, toward his workers was in no way unique among mine owners. Most were despots—and not benevolent ones. In this regard it should be kept in mind that though the prospectors are romanticized, the great bulk of gold and silver came not from panning the streams but from the deep, or "hard-rock," mines, and these were owned by corporations, not miners.

That this should be the case is inevitable given the way gold and silver occur in nature. Gold is found integrated physically though not chemically with quartz, a hard, glasslike mineral. Silver occurs most commonly as a compound, a sulfide. In each case, an elaborate system of machinery is required to tear the metal-bearing rock from the earth, to crush it, and to extract its wealth. The necessary equipment is expensive, requiring a capital investment far beyond the means of the average prospector.

As a consequence, the usual course of events in the West was for a prospector to "strike it rich," to take out what he could with pick, shovel, and pan, and then to sell out his claim for a fraction of its value to someone with the funds to exploit it. The new owner would bring in professional miners, dig shafts and tunnels, and build a mill in which the ore could be processed.

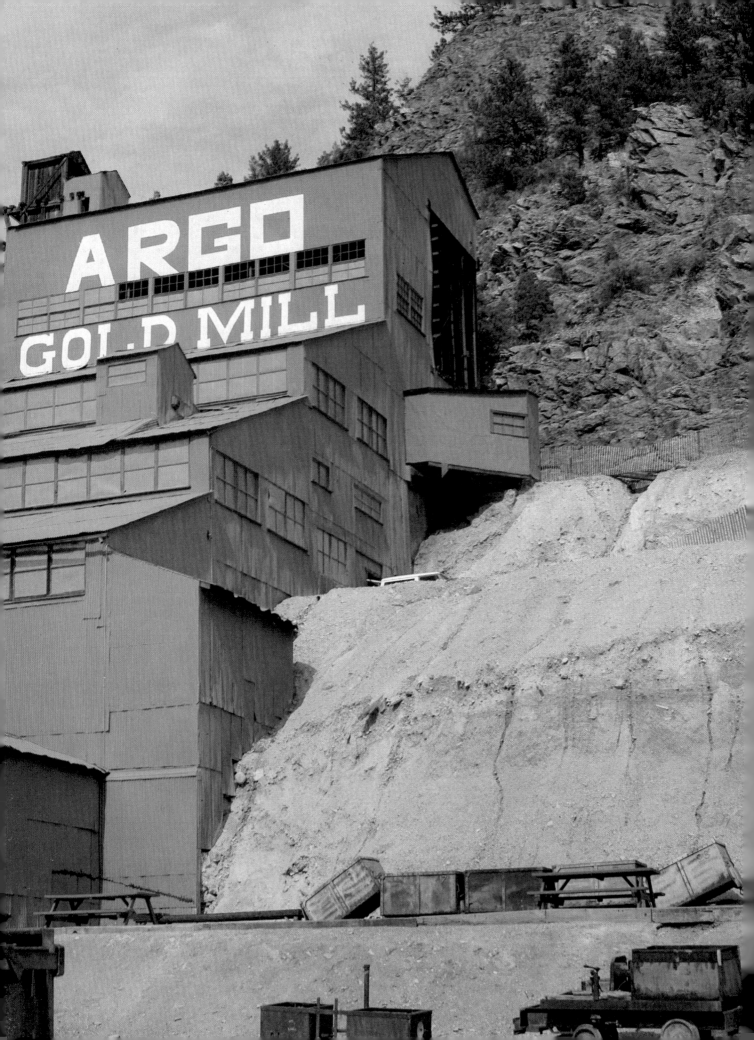

◀

General view of the restored Argo Gold Mill; Idaho Springs, Colo.; active from the turn of the century into the 1960s. At mills like this, gold was extracted from ore. The old Argo buildings now house a mining museum.

Ore car in wood; 1900–20; $750–900. This car is near a ▲ chute from which raw ore was dumped into the cars, which ran on a track similar to a railroad track.

Most mining collectibles come from the mills and deep mines. There are drills, pneumatic and hand, used to drill dynamite holes in the mine walls; the ore buckets and carts or cars in which the blasted rock was hauled; and the elevators with which it was drawn to the surface. From the mills come a variety of crushing devices such as Jaw Crushers and Stamp Mills, concentrating and amalgamating tables to separate precious metals from ore, and a variety of devices for weighing and assaying gold and silver.

Elaborate machinery notwithstanding, the common denominator in the mines was the miner, and it is about him that the legends have grown up. To say his life was hard is to understate the case. It was brutal. On the one hand, his life was in almost constant danger from falling rocks or explosions. On the other, he was frequently cheated and exploited by his boss. In the words of the well-known song, "A Miner's Life":

> Watch the rocks, they're falling daily;
> Careless miners always fail.
> Keep your hand upon the dollar,
> And your eye upon the scale.

Working conditions in the deeper mines defy belief. The Comstock Mine in western Nevada had shafts over a half-mile deep. At that level the air became so foul that the miners' candles burned with a pale-blue flame and men fainted at the cutting walls. And it was hot down there. In the Crown Mine near Virginia City temperatures reached 150 degrees! Huge quantities of ice were lowered into the shafts to cool the men and their tools. Even so, men could work no more than fifteen minutes out of each hour, and hundreds were felled by heat-induced stomach cramps.

Even technical improvement worked against the miners. When pneumatic drills were introduced, they were hailed as a great labor saver; but within a few years men were dying of silicosis produced by the clouds of fine rock dust thrown off by the machines. Only when water cooling was developed did the drills cease to be killers.

Cave-ins and rock falls were a constant menace. Tunnels were not always properly braced, and even when they were, there was always the danger of hitting an area of soft rock or having the bracing disrupted by an improperly set charge. Yet it was not until the early 1900s that the protective mining helmet became standard in the western mines.

One might assume that men would be well paid for working under such extreme conditions, but such was not the case. Miners frequently labored ten hours a day for three to four dollars. They had, in some instances, other ways of making money. Wherever gold was found loose in the tunnels it had a way of ending up in the miner's pocket. "High grading," as it was known, became so prevalent in the western mines that at least one company, that at Wickenburg, Arizona, was forced into bankruptcy by it.

The problem came to a head at Goldfield, Nevada, in 1907, when mine owners introduced "changing rooms," where workers were required to change from work to street clothes under the eyes of the guards. The miners rebelled, and under the leadership of the Industrial Workers of the World, an early union, they struck to end changing and for better working conditions in general. The mine owners (such was their power) brought in federal troops, and a bloody confrontation developed. Eventually the matter was resolved, and, in time, most western mines were unionized.

The miners were eventually brought down by another foe: lack of ore to work. By 1900, most of the western gold and silver claims had been worked out, and, though copper mining remained profitable, the bonanza days were over. For decades the gaping tunnels and abandoned machinery—as well as the ghost towns around them—were nothing but a tourist trap (and a valuable source of mining relics). Now, however, there is a faint stirring of activity. Spurred on by record gold prices and a declining economy, men and women are going back to the mines. There are placers being worked in Nevadaville, Colorado, and new shafts sunk at famous old Cripple Creek. A new breed of prospector, armed with modern equipment, is taking the field. Who can say but that once again the cry of "Gold! Gold on the American River!" will be heard in the streets of San Francisco.

Miners' Tools and Paraphernalia

Although tools specifically related to the craft of mining are relatively few and indistinguished, they are in great demand among collectors. This situation is due in large part to the nature of the occupation.

Mining, be it for gold or copper, requires complex machinery. When, as in the early West, such equipment was not available, the miner resorted to common implements such as the pick, shovel, and sledgehammer. The first men to work the California goldfields did not always have even these tools, yet they took their share of bullion. They were able to do this because the loose ore particles, or placer gold, were mixed with sand in the beds of streams and could easily be separated out by swirling a mixture of earth and water in a flat pan until the lighter materials spilled over the edge of the container leaving the heavier gold flakes or nuggets. At first, whatever pans were available were used, and these included everything from washbasins to frying pans. Soon specifically designed miners' pans became available. These were about eighteen inches in diameter with a gently sloping wall seldom more than three inches high. Made of tin, zinc, or, occasionally, copper, pans were produced in vast quantities throughout the nineteenth century and are still being made. Manufacturer-marked examples are known but uncommon. Since the form of the pans has changed little over the years, it is often difficult to distinguish an 1880s piece from one made during the 1920s.

A shovel was required to remove gold-bearing sand from creek beds, and mining shovels are legitimate collectibles. Unfortunately, most shovels used in mining had no special characteristics to distinguish them from the ordinary garden variety, so lacking a reliable history of use, one can seldom be sure of owning a ''miner's'' shovel. Much the same can be said of the variety of pickaxes and crow- or pry bars that appear in many collections. These were of great importance not only to the miner but also to the builder, the mason, and the railroadman. Again, a history of use in the mines is important.

The use of picks and pry bars reflects a different stage in the evolution of prospecting. As the placer gold became harder to find, prospectors turned to the so-called dry diggings, extracting ore from cracks in rock walls along the streambeds. At first they employed nothing more than a hunting knife or iron spoon for this task, but the pick and crowbar were soon pressed into service, and these accompanied the miner when he at last left the surface veins and began to bore into the living rock.

When he went into the shafts and tunnels, the miner also took with him sledgehammer and ''steel,'' the latter a variety of hand-held iron drill with which holes could be bored into the rock face. The worker placed blasting powder in these cavities in order to shatter the ore-bearing rock. Miners' sledgehammers and drills, like picks and pry bars, are often difficult to distinguish from similar tools used by other workers. This is not the case, however, with the powerful pneumatic drills that were introduced into western mines during the 1880s. They are distinctive equipment and are regarded as highly collectible. The same can be said of the labeled or branded barrels and boxes in which blasting powder was packed.

Other miners' paraphernalia includes cooking and eating utensils, the water barrels and canteens so vital in the dry western wastes and the hot mines, and the bags, or ''pokes,'' in which gold dust and nuggets were transported. In fact, any useful object employed by a prospector or miner is of interest to some collector. Of particular note are pieces marked by mine owners or by makers of mining equipment and commemorative items associated with the field.

View of abandoned mine buildings; Nevadaville, Colo. As ▲ work ceased in the played-out mines, buildings like this were left to decay. Piles of waste rock from the nearby mines can be seen in the background.

Superstructure of mine elevator; central Colorado; the ▶
complete mine elevator, fully restored, would cost
$35,000–50,000. As the mines were dug ever deeper,
complex elevators became necessary to get men and
materials to the lower depths.

Ore car; $550–650. This car is on a track leading to the upper
level of a gold mill. After removal from the mine, ore cars
would be drawn along the track to the mill by a small steam
or electric engine. ▼

◄
Boiler used to power steam-driven mechanisms; Cripple Creek, Colo.; used during the late 1890s; $5,000–6,000. Obsolete locomotives were frequently pressed into service to provide steam for drills and elevators.

Waterwheel; used at the Charles Taylor Mine, Ute Creek, Colo.; 1907–40; a wheel of this period would cost $40,000–50,000 reconstructed. Water was vital to mining operations, for without it precious metals could not be separated from the raw ore. ▼

Prospector's tools; 1900–25. Pan in tin; $35–40. Shovel; ▲ $10–15. Pickax; $15–20. Marked examples of these items would be much more valuable.

Black-and-white photo of hard-rock miners; California; 1900–10; $35–45. Photos of miners ▲ and mining activity are prime collectibles. A daguerreotype would be worth ten times the price of this photo.

Miner's pry or crowbar in hardened steel; 1910–30; $12–18. First used to pry gold from quartz veins in creek beds, the pry bar became an indispensable tool of the underground hard-rock miner. ◀

Commemorative pick and shovel, brass ▲ plated with the monogram of an early Colorado mining company; 1930s; $250–350 the set. The price reflects the premium placed on items of this sort, which were usually made as a gift for a mine officer or employee or to mark the anniversary of a mine opening.

Reverse-glass painting of mine tunnel, ore-car track, and burro; 1940s; $275–350. This painting in black on clear glass is a unique example of western folk art. ▼

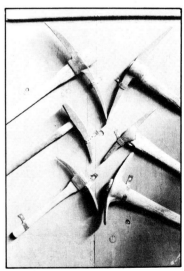

Miners' tools; 1890–1930. ▲ Pickaxes; $15–25 each. Shapes of the axes reflect the various uses to which they were put.

Stenciled blasting-powder box in wood; 1925–40; $25–35. Since it is relatively easy to manufacture, blasting powder was often produced near the mines, but after 1900 most miners obtained their supply from large eastern companies that shipped it in stenciled and sometimes decorated barrels and boxes. ▼

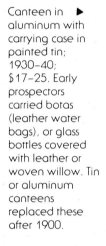

Canteen in ▶ aluminum with carrying case in painted tin; 1930–40; $17–25. Early prospectors carried botas (leather water bags), or glass bottles covered with leather or woven willow. Tin or aluminum canteens replaced these after 1900.

Oilcan in tin; 1920–30; $12–16. Since most mine machinery ▲ required oil, oilcans of many shapes and sizes abounded in the mines and ore mills.

Water barrel in oak bound with iron; 1880–1900; $65–85. So important were water barrels (and water) to the mines that some companies employed a full-time cooper, or barrel maker. ◀

Frying pans in sheet steel; 1890–1910; $9–14 each. Every ▲ prospector carried a frying pan to cook in, and more than one used his to pan gold.

Stenciling tools in aluminum; 1935–45; $6–9 each. Such ▲ stencils were used to mark ore bags and mining equipment. Proper identification of ore and bullion was of great importance, particularly when ore samples were submitted to the assay office.

Hats and Lighting Devices

No items used by miners were of greater importance to their safety and well-being than their protective hats or helmets and their various lighting devices. As to the former, it is surprising, considering the constant danger of rock falls, that protective headgear was introduced comparatively recently. It was not until late in the nineteenth century that metal hats, similar to those worn by combat troops, first appeared in the mines. These new arrivals were steady and dependable, but also heavy and hot. They were soon replaced by helmets of composition fiber and, later, by ones of reinforced plastic. Almost from the beginning, such headpieces had hooks to which a lamp could be attached so that the worker might have light while also keeping both hands free for labor.

Miners' helmets, especially those bearing the monograms of well-known mining companies, are popular collectibles. Older, steel examples are hard to find, but composition and plastic ones are available at reasonable prices.

Lighting devices were also vital to the miner. Once he left the placers and the surface deposits and plunged into the earth, he found himself in complete darkness, often thousands of feet from natural lighting. The artificial lights used by miners provide one of the most interesting areas of mining memorabilia.

The earliest western miners used candles or fat lamps to light their way, and both devices were well known to their predecessors in Europe and eastern North America. One of the most interesting sources of light was the pricket light, or ``sticking tommy,'' which consisted of a wrought-iron or brass rod pointed at one end and curved in upon itself at the other in order to hold a tallow candle. Such a candleholder could be carried in the hand or wedged into a handy crack in the wall. Though they cannot have cast much light, sticking tommies were used for decades. Some were made by local blacksmiths, but most were factory produced, like the Miner's Favorite, which was advertised in the 1903 edition of a St. Louis hardware dealer's catalog and which sold for just one dollar.

Less frequently seen are round tinderbox-candleholder combinations. These consist of a tin box for storing flint, steel, and tinder with a raised circular rim on top to hold a candle. The invention of matches made these devices obsolete, and few were used in the West.

For stronger illumination than that provided by a candle, the miner could employ a spouted tin fat lamp. This looked something like a coffeepot, with a wick laid in its long spout. Animal fat was the usual fuel, and this provided a bright but foul-smelling light. Fat lamps varied from two to four inches in height, and some had hooks so that they could be attached to helmets.

In time the fat lamp gave way to one fueled by whale oil, and this in turn gave way to kerosene. Kerosene was used almost exclusively in larger lanterns intended to light the tunnels and shafts. Individual lighting became the province of the carbide lamp, an efficient and safe device that held sway in the mines until the introduction of battery-powered electric torches in the early twentieth century. The typical carbide lamp is made of brass or steel, is cylindrical, and is about four inches tall. It casts a strong light and can burn much longer than a candle or fat lamp.

The kerosene lanterns used in the mines were similar in shape to those that were used on farms and in homes, but they were frequently heavier in construction and were provided with protective shields to reduce the danger of fire. Few of them were marked, and it is difficult to establish that a given specimen was actually used in the mines.

With the coming of the generator and tunnel-wide electric lighting, the old lighting devices became obsolete, but they continue to offer the collector further insight into the life of the hard-rock miner.

Pricket holder, or "sticking tommy," in wrought iron; 1880–1900; $25–35. Note how candleholder can be driven into a beam or crack in a rock or hung by its hook from any convenient surface. ▼

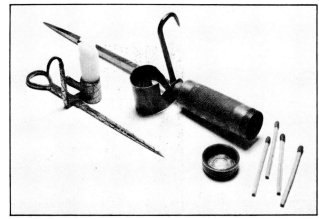

Unusual pricket holders; second half of 19th century. *Left:* ▲ Decorated with scratch carving; $65–80. *Right:* Brass, with a built-in matchbox; $90–110. These are representative of the best in this sort of lighting device.

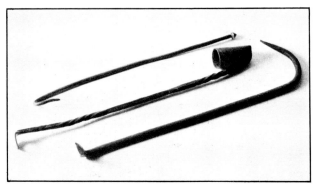

Miners' lighting devices. *Top:* Snuffer with hanging hook; ▲ 1860–75; $40–50. *Center:* Candleholder in wrought iron with twist decoration; 1860–75; $80–95. *Bottom:* Hanger for kerosene lantern in iron; $25–35.

Tinderbox-candleholder combination in sheet tin; 1850–70; $170–190. Though rather indistinguished, tinderboxes are in great demand, hence the rather high price. ◄

Fat lamps; ▶ 1870–90; $45–70. These small (less than 4″ tall) lighting devices were usually attached to the worker's hat by the wrought-metal hook.

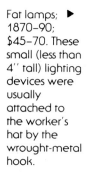

Kerosene lamp in copper and brass; 1870–90; $30–40. ▲ Though seldom used as head lamps, kerosene lighting devices were indispensable for lighting mine tunnels and shafts.

▲ Variety of miners' lighting devices. *Left:* Two carbide lamps in brass; 1890–1920; $45–70 each. *Center:* Kerosene pan lamp in tin; 1880–1900; $20–25. *Right:* Fat lamp in sheet iron; 1870–90; $50–60. From right to left, these devices reflect the steady improvement in mine illumination.

Carbide head lamp in brass; 1890–1910; $55–65. Fueled by carbon, these small lamps provided a strong and safe light for the hard-rock miner. ▼

Mining helmet in steel-reinforced composition; 1930–40; ▲ $35–45. Brass carbide lamp; 1900–20; $55–65. The design of this headgear is similar to that worn in mines today.

Front: Helmet in composition material with original ▲ battery-powered electric head lamp; 1920–30; $75–100. Electric lamps replaced other forms of lighting during the 20th century. *Rear:* Two kerosene lamps used in mine tunnels; 1880–1920; $45–60.

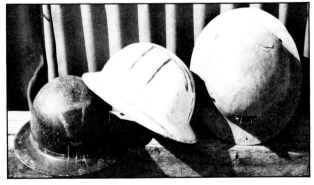

Miners' hats in hard plastic; 1945–60; $20–25. Headgear of this sort is normally not worn in maximum danger areas. ▲

Mining Machinery

Gold was the only metal sought in the West that could commonly be found in a free state on the earth's surface. Silver was usually encountered in a sulfide state, and obtaining copper in profitable quantity involved digging. So as early as the 1860s, miners began to attack the mountain cores in search of their hidden wealth.

Although picks, shovels, and drills were the basic implements employed, profitable exploitation of the mines required machinery that could move and process ore in bulk. This meant large, metal ore buckets, ore cars—which looked like wood or metal boxes on wheels—railwaylike track on which to operate the ore cars, and a whole refining system.

At first, horses and burros or mules were used to haul the ore cars, and the latter, whose braying earned them the name "Rocky Mountain canaries," proved particularly suitable to the arduous task. However, by 1900, battery- or gasoline-driven engines began to take the place of animals, and in time the blacksmith disappeared from a scene to which he had once seemed indispensable.

As the shafts were driven deeper into the living rock, transportation to and from the mine face became more complex and more dangerous. Elevators to carry men, equipment, and ore had to be devised, and power for them had to be provided. At such great depths the strength of humans or animals was of little use, so steam and then electrical hoisting machinery was utilized to raise and lower the metal elevators.

The task did not end when the ore was brought to the surface. It was not, as might be supposed, a great mass of gold, silver, or copper, but rather, for the most part, a nondescript jumble of broken rock. This rubble had to be broken down in order to extract its valuable constituents, and for this purpose, a group of complex machines, housed in a factory called a mill, was employed.

This equipment, belt driven and run by steam or electricity, consisted of such things as Jaw Crushers and Stamp Mills, which reduced foot-square blocks of stone to sand; of mercury amalgamating tables and concentrating tables on which precious metals were separated from the blasted ore; of washing machinery and of chemical retorts in which gold and silver could be reclaimed by a process of distillation.

Every step in the production-line process was calculated to reduce to a minimum the amount of precious metal lost. Yet escape it did, for most authorities agree that between 30 and 70 percent of the gold in reduced ore escaped the miners. There is also a great deal of wealth still in the ground. Some estimate, for example, that less than a third of the gold in the Cripple Creek district in Colorado has so far been recovered. Small wonder, then, that the played-out streams and abandoned shafts of the western mining country are once more alive with prospectors. There is still gold in them thar hills!

Patented adjustable horse or donkey collar in sheet steel; 1900–20; $100–125. These collars were specially designed to deal with the problems involved in hauling ore, and the horse in the photo (*opposite*) is wearing one. ▼

Set of harnesses in leather and wood; 1890–1910; $80–110. Such harnesses were used on burros and horses working the mines. The workers' pride in their beasts of burden is evident in the brass- and glass-decorated tack. ▲

Spikes in wrought iron used in laying ore-car track; ▲ 1880–1930; $4–7 each. Though similar in shape and function to railway spikes, these examples are only 3″ long.

◄

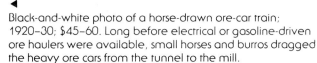

Black-and-white photo of a horse-drawn ore-car train; 1920–30; $45–60. Long before electrical or gasoline-driven ore haulers were available, small horses and burros dragged the heavy ore cars from the tunnel to the mill.

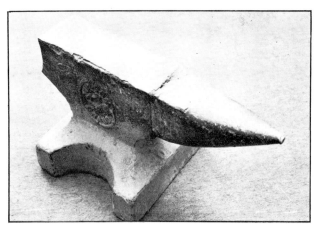

Blacksmith's anvil in wrought iron; 1900–15; $145–225. The need to shoe draft animals and to repair or make a variety of ironware led many mine owners to employ a full-time blacksmith. ▲

155

Blacksmith's charcoal pot in cast iron; 1890–1900; $65–80. ▼

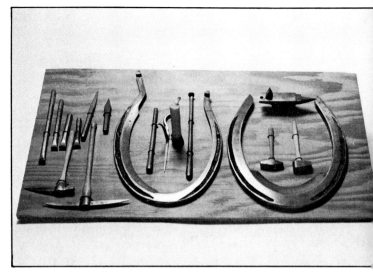

▲
Blacksmith's whimsey of two full-size horseshoes in steel with miniature anvil, sticking tommy, and mining tools; 1920; $175–225. This set was made by an old man who had worked as a blacksmith at several Colorado gold mines.

Mule packsaddle in wrought iron and soft wood; 1870–85; ▶ $125–155. Designed to be worn on the side of the mule, this early and rare saddle is typical of those employed by the first prospectors in the Rockies and California's Sierra.

◀
Heavy-duty supply wagon in wood and cast iron; 1880–1900; $1,400–1,750. Wagons like this carried everything from food and clothing to blasting powder and pig iron to the mines of the western highlands.

◄
Electrically powered
ore train; Argo Gold
Mill, Idaho Springs,
Colo.; 1930s;
$7,000-9,000 in
working order.

Homemade trammer, or ore-car train engine; 1920-30; ▲
$2,400-3,000. This odd-looking device is powered by a
rebuilt engine from a Stanley Steamer automobile.

Battery-powered electric engine; 1910-25; $2,500-3,500 in
working order. Known as a Mancho motor, this engine was
used to pull ore cars through a western mine. ▲

Eimco Mucker; 1930-40; $4,000-5,000 in working order.
This ingenious device was used for scooping up blasted
ore-bearing rock from the mine floor and depositing it in the
ore car directly behind it.
◄

Tractor-mounted air pump used for powering pneumatic
drills; 1935-45; $2,000-2,500 in working order. The
introduction of tools powered by compressed air was a
major technological breakthrough in mining. ▼

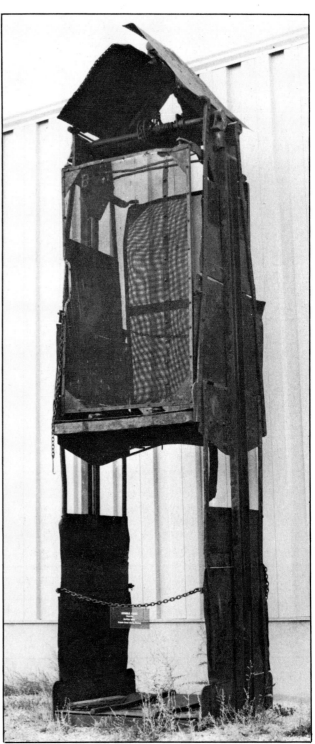

Double-cage mining elevator; used in the Elkton Mine, Cripple Creek, Colo.; 1900–10; $2,000–2,750. Men had to be transported up and down in the mines, and this elevator is typical of those employed. ▼

Ore bucket in cast iron and steel; 1920–40; $80–100. ▲
Smaller buckets were used in ore mills to move the gold-bearing rock from place to place.

Elevator in cast iron and steel; Cripple Creek, Colo.; 1910–20; $1,750–2,500. ▶

Steam-driven hoist; used in the Cressart Mine, Victor, Colo.; 1890–1900; $4,000–5,000 in working order. Such hoists powered the elevators that carried men and ore. ◀

Left: Elevator bell signal; 1920–30; $180–240. *Right:* Bell instruction sign; 1920–30; $160–200. These relatively small objects are choice deep-mine collectibles. ◀

Mine telephone; by Carlson Co.; 1920–30; $175–225. Just as on the railroads, the telephone has played a key role in mining communications. ▶

Arrasta Crusher; 1880–90; $900–1,200. A less efficient device for crushing ore. ◀

Machinery belt; 1910–30; $1–2 for a couple feet. ▲

Slag car in iron; 1880–90; $375–475. Slag cars were used to remove the slag that accumulated during metal smelting. ▶

Assaying Equipment

When his foreman brought John Sutter the first nuggets from California's American River, the old Swiss determined that they were gold by dipping them in nitric acid, a powerful chemical that has no effect on gold or silver. By this act, Sutter became the West's first assayer.

The importance of trained assayers to western mining cannot be underestimated. The first prospectors were barely aware of what gold was, except perhaps in its minted form. They were likely to pick up iron pyrite (''fool's gold'') or even mica and imagine these to be of some value. An even more important function of the assayer was to determine the percentage of precious metal in a vein—although gold and silver could be found in many places, the metals might not be present in sufficient volume to make exploitation profitable. Small wonder, then, that ore mills and most banks (since they regularly trafficked in gold) employed a professional in the field.

Other than his training, the tools of the assayer were few: a mortar and pestle with which to crush the specimens; screens through which to strain them; an oven in which to melt them; and tools and molds with which to handle them and shape them. There were also the scales on which the dust and nuggets were weighed, but these were hardly the exclusive property of the assayer, for in a land where for decades gold was a medium of exchange, nearly every miner, mine or mill owner, banker and storekeeper, owned a set of scales.

The richness of the ore vein, as determined by the assayer, was the key to its development and, often, to its ownership, for wealthy investors waited in the wings to buy up good claims from naive or poverty-stricken prospectors. It is hardly surprising that within months or even weeks of their discovery most of the major western gold and silver lodes were in the hands of wealthy capitalists.

These businessmen quickly incorporated their properties, and today the stock certificates of ownership in these bonanzas are among the most interesting of mining memorabilia. Not all the mines proved profitable. Indeed, many appear to have been opened solely to sell stock to the gullible. So extensive were such schemes that even now gold investment is regarded as risky business at best. Still, the attractive lithographed certificates remain, and, along with deeds to mining claims, they form a historic link with our past.

Assayer's shop sign in lithographed tin; 1910–25; $75–90. ▲

Assayer's tools; 1920–30. *Left:* Ore bag; $20–25. The first ▶ step in assaying ore was to obtain a workable sample, and this would be brought from the mine in an ore bag. *Center:* Sample splitter; $55–70. *Right:* Screen; $45–55.

Mine office sign in black-on-white lithographed tin; Stratton Mine, Cripple Creek, Colo.; 1900–10; $110–140. ▼

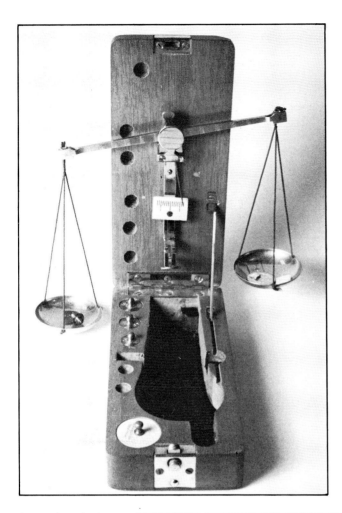

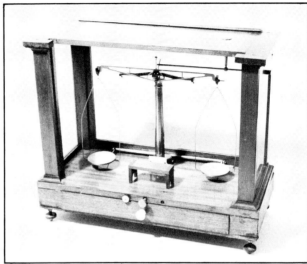

Set of pocket scales in brass; 1880–1910; $110–135. The sort of scales carried by prospectors. ◄

Assayers' or bullion buyers' scales in brass in ▲ mahogany-and-glass case; 1890–1920; $350–425. Every person who bought or tested precious metals had a scale such as this to weigh dust and nuggets.

Assayer's scales in ▶ brass and iron in walnut box with glass slide front; 1870–90; $225–275. Crude and possibly homemade, this scale was intended to be portable.

Very large (nearly 3' high) mortar and pestle; 1890–1900; $150–200. ▼

Mortar and pestle in iron; 1920–30; $70–90. Ore to be assayed was crushed to a fine consistency with a mortar and pestle. ▼

Top: Crucibles in stoneware; 1910–30; $8–22. *Bottom:* Sample ▶ mold in metal; $60–75.

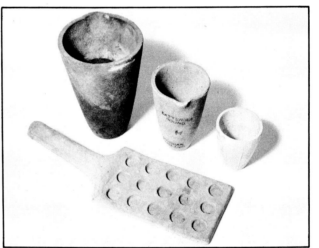

Slag molds from an assay office; 1920–40. *Top:* $50–60. ▲ *Center:* $70–85. *Bottom:* $65–75.

Assayer's tools in iron; 1920–40. *Top:* Crucible holder; ▶ $55–70. *Center:* Ladle for molten metal; $35–45. *Bottom:* Pincers; $50–60.

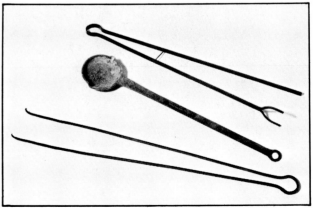

Stock certificate; Bull Hill and Straub Mountain Gold Mining and Milling Co., Colorado; 1903; $8–12. Since nearly all deep mines were held by corporations rather than individuals, trade in gold shares became a major investment field. ▼

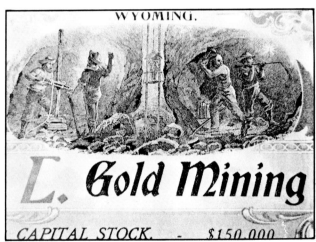

Detail of stock certificate; Wyoming gold mining company; 1901; $16–20. Note that the miners are using hand and pneumatic drills and do not wear protective headgear. Stock certificates can be valuable research tools in the study of mining. ◀

Stock certificates for Colorado gold mines; $8–12 each. ▲ *Left:* St. Thomas; 1901. *Center:* Bull Hill; 1895. *Right:* Woman's; 1894. Availability, inexpensiveness, and interesting graphic design make such certificates great favorites with collectors.

◀

Deeds to western mining lands; $4–7 each. *Left:* 1896. *Center:* 1898. *Right:* 1922. Though historically important, land deeds to mining claims are not sufficiently attractive to appeal to many collectors.

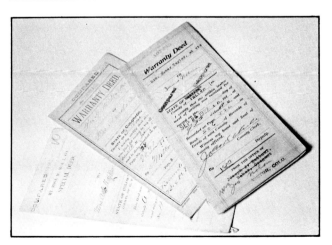

6.

The Iron Road

There have always been collectors of railroadiana. Indeed, it was the efforts of early "collectors," most of whom were railroad employees, that led companies to mark their tools and equipment with their company names. However, the major impetus to the hobby was provided by the great dispersal sales of the early 1970s, when financially troubled companies such as the Penn-Central sold off large quantities of surplus material. The Pennsylvania Railroad auction in 1971, for example, realized over $150,000 in sales of train models, dining-car glass and silver, and advertising materials and flooded the market with a vast quantity of collectibles. Collectibles breed collectors, and today railroad memorabilia is one of the major areas of Americana.

Railroading in general is one thing—the western rails are quite another. In no area of the country did the rails play a greater role than in the West, and nowhere is there, today, greater nostalgia for railroadiana.

But the iron monsters came late to the West. Proposals had been made for the construction of a transcontinental rail line as early as the 1840s, but it was not until 1852 that any track was laid west of the Mississippi. And though the population of California boomed following the gold strike of '49, there were no rails at all there until the completion of the Sacramento-Folsom line in 1856. Still, the impossible dream of uniting the two coasts persisted.

In 1862 Congress passed the first Pacific Railroad Act, which granted charters to two lines: the Central Pacific, which was to build east across the mountains from Sacramento; and the Union Pacific, which was to bridge the deserts west from Omaha. The goal was a linkup somewhere near the California line.

All this would cost a great deal of money, of course, so Congress, which had first started awarding land grants to railways in the 1850s, provided a gift of ten sections of federal land per mile of track laid as well as substantial loans. When little work was done and little private capital was attracted, these terms were bettered in 1864, but by that time the Civil War had effectively halted all construction.

With the coming of peace in 1865, the great project was resumed, and the railway armies swarmed forward. And armies they were, in both numbers and organization. Each line employed between six and ten thousand workers, directed by former Army officers and divided into crews of surveyors, bridge builders, graders, tie men, and track layers. All these operations were carried out with the precision of armies and the workers were supplied like advancing armies, but the builders proved barely equal to the task, for before them lay some of the most difficult country in the world.

The Union Pacific had to contend with blazing heat, dust, lack of water, lack of wood for both fuel and railroad ties, winters so cold that locomotive water tanks froze solid, and, perhaps worst of all, hostile Indians. The Plains tribes rightly viewed the iron monsters as the ultimate weapon in their own subjugation, and they fought them relentlessly. From Nebraska to Utah the war raged. Outmanned and outgunned, the Indians were never outfought. They would sweep down out of the hills, scatter stock, cut telegraph lines, and murder surveying parties. Then they would vanish as quickly as they had come. The toll taken in men killed and time lost was high. It is said that one worker died for every mile of track laid, and in Nebraska and Colorado the line was delayed for weeks at a time because the safety of crews could not be assured.

The Sioux and the Cheyenne were the Indians most feared. In August 1867 the Cheyenne chieftain Turkey Leg, with a few dozen followers, fell upon the line at Lexington, Nebraska, blocking the track with logs, killing a work crew, and derailing the scheduled train. Then, for four days the braves held the track, pillaging and burning freight cars and preventing any westward movement. Only the arrival of federal troops enabled the crews to continue their westward march. So serious were such attacks that at any given time only half the work crews were engaged in work on the rails. The rest were standing guard or pursuing Indian war parties!

Further west things were going no better, though there the enemy was nature rather than men. The Sierra

Preceding pages: Caboose and passenger car used on the Colorado and Southern; 1882; the caboose could be worth as much as $8,000–9,500 restored: the coach might bring $20,000–25,000 restored.

Nevada rears up like a wall on the eastern edge of California. There is no way around, so the Central Pacific had to go over the top, even in winter, when supply trains were blocked by twenty-foot drifts and whole work crews were swept away by snowslides.

Up and up the tracks went until at last they faced a sheer block of granite, a thousand feet high. Dubbed "Cape Horn" by the workers, it seemed an impossible barrier. But the Central engineers were undaunted. They lowered six hundred chisel men on ropes and hacked out a path around the summit. The way cleared, the Central Pacific rolled over the Sierra, dynamiting its way through obstacles, building forty miles of snowsheds to protect its trains from the drifts, and, in 1868, breaking out at last above the eastern desert.

After that it was relatively easy. The rival companies raced across Utah, laying as much as ten miles of track a day and vying for the opportunity to serve Salt Lake City, then the only major community in the area. The rivalry became more heated, spurred on by bonuses and a certain racial rivalry resulting from the fact that the eastern crew was primarily Irish in composition, while that from the West was composed almost entirely of Chinese.

The contest became so frenzied that while their track men were still miles back, the surveyors and grading crews of the competing lines had actually passed each other and were threatening to lay miles of useless parallel trackage. Fortunately, cooler heads prevailed, and it was agreed to join the lines at Promontory Point, Utah. There, on May 10, 1869, a golden spike was driven to bind the last rail to the last tie. The nation finally had a transcontinental railway.

But, of course, driving that golden spike was just the beginning of railroading in the West. The central Pacific coast had its line, but to the north and south there were growing population centers clamoring for access to the eastern markets. They, too, were to have their railroads.

In 1862 the Kansas Pacific started laying track west from Kansas City. When the line reached Abilene, Kansas, in 1865, it revolutionized life in the Southwest. For example, it brought about the great age of the buffalo hunters. Hide merchants had long been seeking an outlet for their leather, and by the hundreds they flocked to Abilene to fill the freight cars with buffalo hides and bone, the latter to be ground into fertilizer.

The buffalo did not last; the cattle did. In Texas, at the close of the Civil War, the ranges were filled with thousands of half-wild longhorn cattle, a rich source of beef for the East. As soon as there was a depot in Abilene, the cattle drives started up the Chisholm Trail. In 1865 alone, 350,000 steers passed through the town.

However, the Kansas Pacific failed to prosper over the long haul, being eclipsed in time by the greatest of all southwestern railways, the Santa Fe. Chartered in 1859 as the Atchison and Topeka Railroad and rechartered in 1863 as the Atchison, Topeka & Santa Fe, the Santa Fe was a late bloomer. It didn't even start to build west of Topeka until 1868, but, when it reached Dodge City in 1873, it stole the cattle trade from Kansas Pacific; and when it built into San Diego in 1885, it established the first southern transcontinental route.

At the roof of the country, the Northern Pacific was chartered in 1864 with the largest land grant in railroading history—a total of 25,600 acres for every mile of track laid! Despite this largesse, the line did not prosper, and it was not until 1883 that the Northern Pacific finally pushed through to the coast.

Many of the Northern Pacific's problems were the result of mismanagement, but some of the blame for the line's difficulties lay with the country through which the rails were run. The Cascade Mountains are not only high—they are also plagued by some of the worst weather imaginable: torrential rainstorms and winter blizzards of epic proportions. A good example of the problems encountered in this country as well as of the courage and tenacity of the railway builders is the construction of the Stampede Tunnel.

When the Northern Pacific first reached Yakima, Washington, it was by way of switchbacks over Stampede Pass. But within a year it became evident that the weather on the peak was too severe to permit continued use. Trains were snowed in or flooded out. Landslides tumbled over the right-of-way. The only solution was a tunnel, a tunnel through two miles of solid rock! The impossible was done. After twenty-eight months and at the cost of a dozen lives, the job was finished.

Courage is one thing, good management another. The Northern Pacific always seemed short on the latter, and bankruptcy became almost a yearly occurrence on the line. When a new rival, the Great Northern, rolled into Everett, Washington, in 1893, it was only a matter of time before the Northern Pacific went into receivership.

Further south something new appeared on the scene: the narrow-gauge railroads. At an early date the eastern lines had standardized track width at four feet eight and one-half inches, thus making it possible for all equipment to use all trackage. In Colorado, however, the abundance of mountains and the need to service small but rich mining towns in those mountains led to the establishment of narrow-gauge lines with tracks only three feet across. The most famous of all these was the Denver & Rio Grande, chartered in 1870.

The Denver & Rio Grande was famous for a lot of things: for its war with the Santa Fe for right-of-way through the picturesque Royal Gorge, a real conflict in which men died and miniature forts dotted the rugged river valley; for its continued use of narrow-gauge roads on most branches until the 1950s; and for its employment of the "Galloping Geese," gasoline-powered trucks that ran on the rails and carried mail into the fastnesses of the Rockies. No history of western railroading could be complete without reference to the "baby railroads" of Colorado.

Nor would the story be told adequately without some mention of the accidents and the outlaws that plagued the western lines.

Contrary to what one would expect given the rugged terrain over which the western rails ran, the accidents on the western roads have never compared with those in the East. Perhaps this is due to less congested schedules; perhaps just to good luck. Yet, as might be expected, the accidents that did occur were spectacular and, sadly enough, all too often were due to human error. For example, it was only six months after the spike was driven at Promontory Point when a switchman on the Western Pacific line north of San Francisco was given written orders to reset some switches to accommodate a late-running passenger train. The orders were complete and accurate. Unfortunately, the switchman had never learned to read. The passenger train hit a freight at fifty miles per hour, and sixteen people died.

Then, in March 1906, a local telegrapher dozed at his chair while his machine tapped out an order change to sidetrack the local train while an oncoming express cleared the station. The message went unheard, and the express plowed into the local near the Royal Gorge in western Colorado. Fire broke out, and thirty-five passengers were lost.

But the worst of the western tragedies occurred without fault. Late in the day on August 4, 1904, a sudden downpour flooded Hogan's Gulch on the Denver & Rio Grande line north of Pueblo, Colorado. The rain-weakened bridge gave way, and a southbound train from Denver plunged into the stream taking with it ninety-seven people. There was an ironic postscript to this accident. Months later, a local farmer found the body of one of the victims and decided to hold it for a reward. Neighbors found this unique form of kidnapping repugnant and suggested a "necktie party" might be appropriate. The farmer hastily gave up his prize.

Of course, if there are trains, there must be train robbers. Given the aura of mystery and romance surrounding them, the men who held up the western trains are viewed by many as the most successful as well as the most exciting of all felons. This, however, is not the case. Most train robbers were both incompetent and unsuccessful. True, there were Butch Cassidy and the Sundance Kid, who, operating out of their hide-out at Hole in the Wall, Wyoming, specialized in robbing the Union Pacific and took off with over a hundred thousand dollars at the turn of the century. But they were unusual. A lot more common were men like the Jennings gang of Oklahoma. Their first attempt was aborted when they were run off by a sixty-five-year-old conductor waving a red lantern. The next time they made a play it was for the Missouri, Kansas & Texas near Edmond, Oklahoma. They piled timber on the track. The train ran over the pile and went on its way. When the Jennings bunch finally did stop a train, they collected all of $300. True, there were a couple of safes aboard, and the gang had dynamite. They just didn't know how to use it. They blew the side out of a freight car and blasted the car off the tracks, but they never dented the safes.

There were also the James brothers. They took their first train in 1873, derailing it by cutting loose a rail and pulling it out of line with a rope as the train approached. They got $10,000 for their trouble, but their next several efforts netted less than $2,000, and the James boys went back to robbing banks. Other notorious train robbers were Sam Bass, who took $60,000 in gold off a train at Big Springs, Nebraska (probably the best haul ever), and the Daltons, who operated in Oklahoma during the 1890s. For the most part, though, the great train robbers came on the scene late and could never accommodate their techniques to changing times and more sophisticated law enforcement.

The legends of the western railways go on and on: the paddys "who worked on the railway" for fifty cents a day and all the hardships they could endure; the brave engineers like Casey Jones "who died in the wreck with his hand on the throttle" rather than endanger others; the ruthless magnates like Jay Gould and Cornelius Vanderbilt (whose motto was "the public be damned"), who used rail lines like chess pieces in a nationwide game of high finance. All these and more went to make up the western roads, and those who today collect railroad memorabilia hold a part, albeit a small one, of that great and fruitful dream.

Rolling Stock

The idea of collecting railroad locomotives or cars may seem bizarre. After all, many of these monsters weigh up to twenty tons or more, making transportation and storage very difficult. There is also the matter of expense. Although junked locomotives have sold for a few thousand dollars in cash and cars have sold for much less, the costs of restoration are gigantic, pushing the value of restored rolling stock well into the tens of thousands of dollars.

Nevertheless, collectors there are. Most of them are railroad museums or businesses such as restaurants, nightclubs, and specialty shops that find the old vehicles make eye-catching attractions. Such collectors account for most sales, but there are also a few individuals who delight in owning a caboose or a ''tiny'' eight-ton narrow-gauge engine.

Locomotives are the top of the heap, though they are considerably less practical than more mundane stock, such as freight and passenger cars. Though a few earlier examples may be found, most collectible engines were made after 1870.

The earliest locomotives were little more than wheel-mounted steam boilers, and even in the 1830s a typical example might weigh no more than five tons. Yet even then they had power to excite the imagination. The clanking, flame-spouting and smoke-bellowing machines were so unlike anything previously seen that they drew crowds wherever they appeared. When the designer Peter Cooper raced his diminutive *Tom Thumb* against an equally burdened wagon team in 1830, a throng of thousands watched the match. The results were mixed. The little engine reached a speed of eighteen miles per hour and was clearly outdistancing its rival—when it broke down. Partisans of faithful dobbin hooted with derision and sighed in relief, but wiser men sided with Baltimore & Ohio engineer Horatio Allen when he observed: ''In the future there is no reason to expect any material improvement in the breed of horses, while in my judgment the man is not living who knows what the breed of locomotive is to command.''

In just a few short years, American ingenuity proved Allen a prophet. The first standardized locomotives used in this country were of British make, the so-called Planet class, but these engines, designed as they were for the plains and low hills of England, proved inadequate in the broken country of the Northeast. More power was needed, and this meant more driving wheels than the two employed on the imported engines. Accordingly, in 1836 Henry Campbell, chief engineer of the Germantown railway, patented an eight-wheeled locomotive with four driving wheels preceded by a four-wheel truck. Denominated the ''4-4-0,'' this engine became so popular that it was soon called ''the American type,'' and over twenty-five thousand were manufactured, many of which served in the western states where they were used until the end of the nineteenth century.

But as the railheads were pushed west, the great plains and high mountains that were encountered called for even more power. By the 1880s, gargantuan 4-8-0s, with eight driving wheels, were forcing their way through the Rocky Mountain passes. There were other variations: the popular 4-6-0, the 2-8-0, and even a monster 4-10-0, but none was as popular as the basic design.

The first engines were wood burners, but following the Civil War the lines that pushed west employed coal wherever possible. In fact, the coal-burning steamer was the standard for the railway industry until well into this century. Thomas Edison demonstrated an electric engine in 1880, and electricity proved popular for street railways, or trolleys. Electric engines were also used in the so-called Eastern Corridor, from Boston to Washington, where there was great objection to both the smoke and the noise of the big boilers. However, the real foe of the steam locomotive was diesel, introduced in 1928 and dominant twenty years later. Today few steamers can be found other than on seasonal tourist roads, but for most collectors memorabilia of the steam era is the desired acquisition.

Oddly enough, advances in railway-car design lagged far behind engine technology. The first passenger cars looked like just what they were intended to replace—stagecoaches—and though these were soon replaced by wooden compartments, most efforts were directed at producing more efficient freight carriers. For decades travelers endured hard wood seats, dangerous lighting, and inadequate heat.

All this changed with the appearance of George M. Pullman. In 1865, Pullman's factory built the first luxury coach, the Pioneer, at a cost of better than $20,000.

With its walnut-and-marble interior, plush chairs, and oil-burning chandeliers, the Pioneer was an immediate hit with the well to do. By 1876 Pullman cars had a hot-water heating system and resembled moving hotels.

Pullman didn't stop there. In 1868 he put into service the first dining car, appropriately called the Delmonico, after the great New York restaurant. Pullman thus put an end to the days when passengers carried their own food or scrambled off trains at brief station stops to grab a snack in the local greasy spoon.

Parlor cars with reclining seats and observation cars appeared in the 1870s, making transcontinental travel one of that period's great luxuries.

Freight cars, too, were rapidly diversified. Soon after 1865 standard box- and flatcars were joined by rudimentary freezer compartments and hopper cars for everything from grain to coal. And there were always cabooses. Serving as home, office, and restaurant for freight-train crews, these odd little tagalongs have survived in substantial numbers and are among the most popular collectible cars.

Steam locomotive of the 2–8–0 type; built by the Baldwin works; 1880; $60,000 ▲ restored. This engine was used for years on the Denver, South Platte & Pacific before ending its days in 1932 as a log hauler in a Wisconsin lumber camp. Many aging engines were utilized in mining and lumber camps or as freight switchers.

Abandoned cast-iron wheel truck of the sort widely employed throughout the West; late 19th century. Restorers offer as much as $250–400 for similar parts.

View of the rear platform of a Union Pacific observation car; ca. 1900; $30,000–40,000 restored. The cast-iron grillwork is enhanced by brass fittings characteristic of the period.

Detailed view of the firebox door of Engine 583; 1890. Engine 583 could bring $25,000–40,000 in restored condition. One of the last great steamers, this engine was used on the Denver & Rio Grande as well as on the San Luis Valley Southern, where it was active until 1956.

A "Galloping Goose"; put into service in 1931 and retired 11 ▲
years later; $7,000–9,500 restored. Powered by a Buick en-
gine and specially designed to run on the narrow-gauge
track employed by the Rio Grande Southern, these vehicles
were intended primarily for mail runs, but they could also
carry passengers.

Interior of a Denver & Rio Grande passenger car; built in   ▶
1880 and used until 1940; $20,000–25,000 restored. This
car, which was used on the Denver to Santa Fe run, is typical
of the wood-bodied cars used in the 19th century. After
several serious fires, the western railroads began to employ
steel-bodied passenger cars, though older models continued
in use until retired.

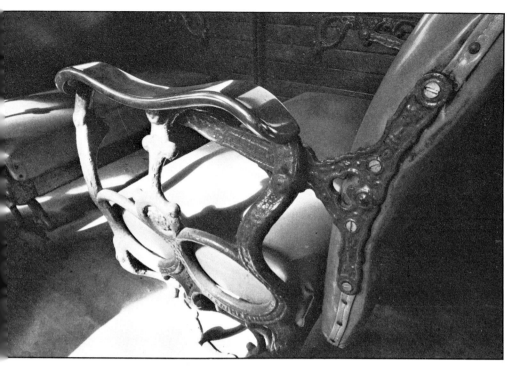

Detail of cast-iron reclining coach seat with stainless-steel armrest; by G. Buntin, Boston, Mass.; patented 1867; $125–175.
◄

Cast-iron and tin railway sink and water fountain in place in caboose; early 20th century; worth $145–185 to a restorer. These objects reflect the "comforts of home" as available to a typical train crew.
▼

Cast-iron and steel railway stove in place in caboose; 1902; $275–350. This stove was still in use as late as 1951.
◄

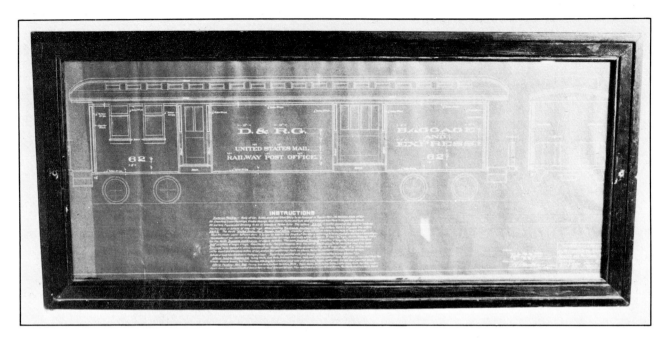

Blueprint for railway post-office car; dated 1904; $75–95. ▲
Such plans are always of interest to collectors of railroad
paper and documents.

Logbook giving locomotive oil changes for engines operating on the Denver & Royal Gorge; 1911; $55–70. While of
historical importance, such logs appeal only to a limited
number of collectors. ▶

Motor inspection board for Rio Grande Southern Galloping
Goose motorcars; 1930–40; $80–110. Constant inspection
was a key to safety on the western roads, and boards like
this one enabled personnel to maintain the necessary
records. ▶

Stainless-steel bell of Engine 318, a Rio Grande locomotive; 1896; $350–475. This engine was used at Cripple Creek, Colo., during the bitter labor disputes there. The engine still bears the marks of bullets fired at it by union pickets. Railroad bells are popular with collectors. ▼

Steel locomotive number plate for a Union Pacific Chal- ▲ lenger Class (4–6–6–4) locomotive; 1935–40; $350–450. Though a prestigious collector's piece, the engine number usually tells the sad tale of another old locomotive cut up for scrap.

Locomotive number plate in cast iron for a Rio Grande & ▲ Southern engine (4-6-0); 1916–42; $545–625. The locomotive that bore this plate was a narrow-gauger used in the Rocky Mountains, one of the most rugged places in which a train could be operated.

Aluminum brake covers and cover with handle; 1945–55; $15–20 each. Such items are typical of the specialized collectibles available to the railroad buff. ▼

Brass and cast-iron passengers' chime whistle from a Denver ▲ & Rio Grande narrow-gauge locomotive; 1910–20; $185–235. Whistles are an important part of railway lore. Every early engineer had his whistle made to order; eventually, everyone along the right-of-way could tell who was at the throttle by the whistle's tone, or "moan."

Lighting Devices

Both because of their ready availability and because of general interest in the field of lighting, lamps and lanterns, both exterior and interior, are among the most popular of railroad memorabilia. Workmen's lanterns are the easiest pieces to come by, but the larger engine and signal lamps are in greater demand.

Trains were not always lighted. At first the problem of lighting was avoided by operating trains only during daylight hours. But with longer runs and increasing patronage, nighttime travel became mandatory, and various lighting devices began to appear. The first of these were larger versions of traditional stagecoach lights: fat lamps or candles set behind glass shades. It soon became evident, however, that a train traveling fifteen or twenty miles per hour needed a more powerful headlight, and various expediencies were resorted to, including pine-knot fires set on a platform before the engineer's box.

Candles and open fires were unreliable and a bad thing, indeed, in a time when everything from a herd of bison to a landslide might be encountered along the right-of-way. Nevertheless, until the introduction of kerosene, in 1859, most engine headlights were fueled by whale oil or by the highly inflammable burning fluid camphene. With large reflectors, kerosene lamps could do a serviceable job in open country, but something better was required for the deep tunnels and sharp curves of the western mountains. This was provided by the introduction in 1881 of electric lamps. Most collectible engine and signal lights are kerosene or electric, but there are also a few gas-powered versions, which reflect the use of this medium in the late nineteenth century.

Interior lighting was viewed as less important than exterior lighting because it was not so directly related to railroad safety. Therefore, until the 1840s many lines provided no interior lighting. Passengers brought their own candles in glass-covered holders. After a few nasty fires, the railroads decided that they should provide the candles and house them in special glass-enclosed wall sockets. In the 1850s these were replaced by kerosene or whale-oil lamps, and around 1875 a further refinement in the form of illuminating gas was introduced. But the threat of fire remained. Dozens of passengers burned to death following relatively minor train wrecks simply because ruptured kerosene or gas lamps ignited coach interiors. Fortunately, this risk was greatly reduced with the electrification of most coaches after 1887.

Perhaps the most important lights from the point of view of the general collector are those used for signaling, whether on the train or by various railroad personnel. All locomotives carried a variety of marker lamps that indicated what action the train was taking or the direction in which it was moving. Most of such lights were affixed to the front and sides of the engine, with some at its rear or on the tender or caboose. In days when most train signals had to be transmitted visually or by whistle, these lights were a critical safety factor.

Equally important were the signal lamps affixed to track switches, which indicated the direction in which a switch had been thrown or instructions as to how an oncoming train should proceed. During the day similar information was conveyed by metal semaphore, just as flags displayed on the locomotives paralleled the function of the running lights.

Finally there are the many different hand lamps used by conductors, brakemen, and switchmen. The earliest of these were fueled by fat or whale oil, but most seen in contemporary collections are of the familiar kerosene or battery-powered type. These may have clear- or colored-glass shades. One of the most appealing aspects of such hand lamps is that many are marked (usually on the metal frame) with the name of the railroad on which they were used. Lanterns from lines that have gone out of operation are especially desirable, as are the commemorative lamps given to retiring employees.

Railroad headlamp of ▲ lithographed tin and sheet steel; 1870–80; $650–750. This kerosene engine lamp still bears its original lithographed decoration. It was used on the Denver, South Park & Pacific and is over 3' high.

Engine headlamp of ▲ japanned black tin and sheet steel; Southwest; 1875–85; $500–575. Kerosene lamps such as this threw only a fitful light in the dark mountain passes of the West.

Railroad marker light of sheet ▲ steel and cast iron; 1900–30; $275–350. Lights such as this were attached to the locomotive or caboose to indicate the action a train was taking.

Switch-stand lamp of sheet ▶ steel and cast iron combined with red and white semaphore; by Deitz; 1920–30; $600–700. Mounted on the station house, this signal advised incoming trains as to whether or not the station was clear.

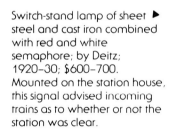

Railroad switch-stand lamp of ▲ sheet steel and cast iron with red and green lenses; 1910–20; $250–325. Early switching lamps were kerosene, but most collectible examples are electrical.

Switching signal generator in steel; by Union Switch and Signal Co.; ca. 1902; $155–185. Small generators such as this powered individual switches all along the western roads. ◀

Cloth signal flags; 1930–40; $15–25 each. Flags such as these were displayed on the engine during daylight hours to show the type of train, what it was carrying, and if it was followed by other sections. ▼

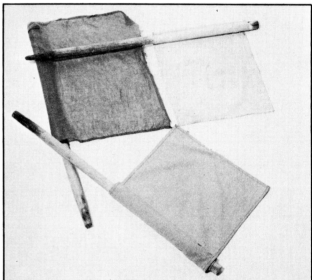

Tin flag case with red brakeman's flag; used on and marked by the Wabash; 1935–45; $135–160. While signal flags are quite common, old flag cases are hard to come by. ▼

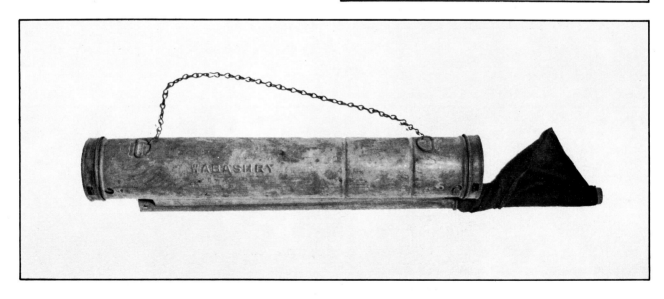

Preceding pages: Steam engine of the Rio Grande & Southern; built in 1899 and used until 1951; $65,000–70,000 restored. This 42-ton narrow-gauge locomotive is shown drawing freight.

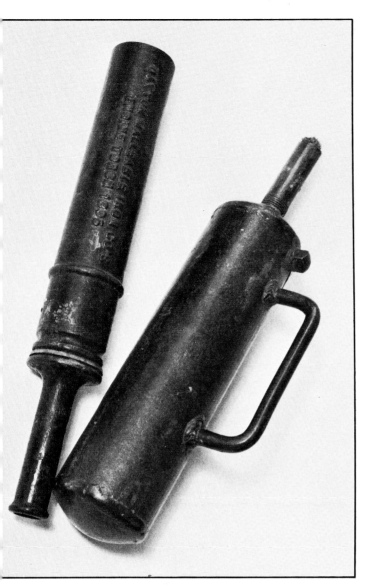

Cast-iron locomotive torches. *Left:* By Dayton Malleable Iron Co.; dated 1895; $50-60. *Right:* 1910-25; $15-20. Railroad torches were used to signal as well as to mark parked or disabled stock.
◀

Hand lanterns; 1910-30; $60-65 each. *Left:* Red with clear glass; marked by Union Pacific. *Right:* Black with orange-tinted shade; marked by Denver & Southern. ▲

◀

Railroad lamp in sheet steel painted black; by Handlan, St. Louis, Mo.; 1920-30; $165-210. This kerosene lamp is particularly attractive.

Refrigerator car with wooden frame; 1920–30; ▶
$6,000–7,000. Refrigerator cars were put into service soon
after the Civil War, but it was many years before they were
perfected.

"Pee Wee" narrow-gauge locomotive; by Baldwin
Locomotive Works, Philadelphia, Pa.; ca. 1900; with a
late-19th-century all-wood caboose; $25,000–30,000 for
locomotive and caboose. It was not until the 1900s that steel
fully replaced wood in train construction. ▼

Steam locomotive, Manitou & Pikes Peak; 1900–20; ▲
$40,000–45,000 fully restored. Specially designed
cog-wheel trains ran on a track and pinion line that climbed
Colorado's 14,000-foot Pikes Peak.

Hand lamps; 1930–40; $25–35 each. *Left:* Aluminum ▶
carbide lamp; by Oxwell. *Right:* Blue-glass battery-powered
lamp. These lamps are the result of the switch from kerosene
during the 20th century.

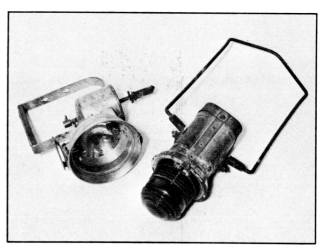

Presentation lantern in electroplated silver; 1930s; ▲
$200–275. Presentation lanterns were given to retiring
railroad employees and are quite rare.

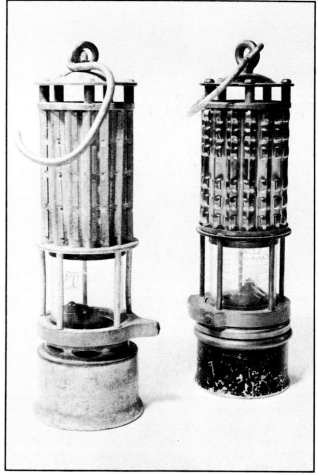

Safety lamps; 1910–30. *Left:* Aluminum; $50–65. *Right:* ▲
With brass screen; $70–85. Safety lamps were used
whenever there was danger of encountering explosive
gases. They are somewhat uncommon.

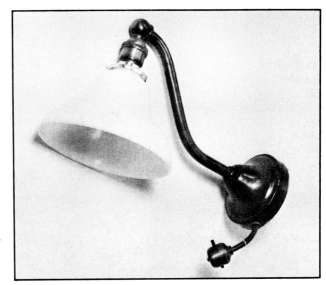

Station house or vestibule light of brass plate and milk glass; ▶
1930–45; $45–50. Many lights of this sort are still in use.

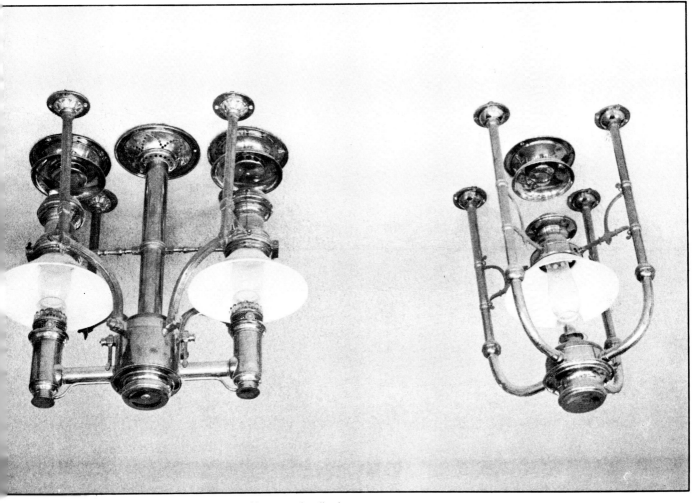

Kerosene dining-room ceiling lamps of brass and milk glass; ▲
1880–1900. *Left:* Double light with punch decoration;
$750–825. *Right:* Single light; $475–575. Lights of this sort
embellished the palatial dining cars of the late Victorian era.
Today they are in great demand for restaurant and
boutique lighting.

Electrified trolley car, Fort Collins, Colo., Municipal Railway; 1930–50; $14,000–16,000 restored. Electrification was more common with trolleys than with trains. In the background is a restored station.

Trolley car in wood and steel, Denver & Intermountain; built in Denver, Colo.; 1911; $11,000–12,500. This trolley operated until 1953, running between Denver and Golden, Colo. Its lifetime spans the period during which trolleys were an important form of transportation. ▼

Telegraph line; northern New Mexico. The telegraph was critical to the operation of the early railroads, and today telegraph and telephone insulators are eagerly sought by collectors. ◀

Station sign in lithographed sheet steel, Colorado and ▲ Southern; 1950–60; $65–80. As trains and lines are discontinued, railroad signs are becoming popular collectibles.

Railroad Workers' Clothing and Equipment

From the spic-and-span uniforms of the conductors to the oilcans and toolboxes of the yardmen who kept the trains running, clothing and equipment are among the most varied and interesting of all railroad collectibles. Many types of objects are available, and—best of all—most of them are relatively inexpensive.

Items of clothing are especially collectible because they are for the most part small and easily displayed. Chief among these are the caps worn by conductors, brakemen, and other employees who dealt directly with the public. Such headgear is enhanced by the fact that most examples are embroidered with the employee's position and the name of the line for which he worked. It should be noted, though, that few pre-1890 caps can be found, for it was late in the nineteenth century before railroads adopted uniforms for their employees. Before that, the railroader looked pretty much like his passengers, a situation that led to all sorts of misunderstandings.

Caps were often adorned with brass- or nickel-plated badges, and these badges form a separate area for the collector. The copper-alloy or aluminum buttons that were used on uniforms are also very collectible. Like cap badges, uniform buttons usually bear a company's name or initials. Buttons vary in size, depending upon whether they were worn on coat fronts, cuffs, or caps, and they appear in great variety. Trainmen were not the only employees to wear uniforms with special buttons; trolley, horsecar, and subway employees all had their own uniforms with their own buttons. Button collections that include hundreds or even thousands of examples are not unknown.

Somewhat different in form are lapel buttons and pins, which look somewhat like miniature badges and were primarily decorative.

Some people collect the actual uniforms, the coats and trousers. The most desirable are the earliest (pre-1900) and those that bear embroidered railway labels. Since most uniforms were dark blue and standardized in shape, they are not particularly interesting without the appropriate badges, buttons, and so forth.

Because of the dangers of tampering or theft, railroads have long protected switches, call boxes, and equipment shanties with heavy brass or iron padlocks. Keys to these were issued to appropriate employees. Both locks and keys are customarily stamped with the name of the issuing line, and collectors in this area strive to obtain matching, marked sets, preferably from defunct lines.

The problem of theft extended to such mundane things as water cans and oilcans; therefore many of these are marked with company names and are prime collectibles. More personal are the tools with which maintenance men worked, and among these toolboxes are particularly valued because they were often made by the worker himself and may bear his name.

Generally issued items that have interest for the railroad buff include first-aid kits, especially those used on the wrecking trains that were sent to the scene of accidents; fire extinguishers; stencils for marking boxcars; and the iron spikes that bound together ties and tracking. There are so many different types of spikes, many of which are stamped with the initials of the line on which they were used, that some collectors confine themselves to this area of railroadiana. Fortunately, except for the rare examples, railway spikes are inexpensive.

Somewhat more difficult to obtain and much harder to store or display are larger pieces of railroad maintenance equipment. These include hand-powered or electric cars used to transport crews along the right-of-way, firefighting equipment, and larger steam-cleaning paraphernalia. Most pieces of this sort are purchased for museums or restorations.

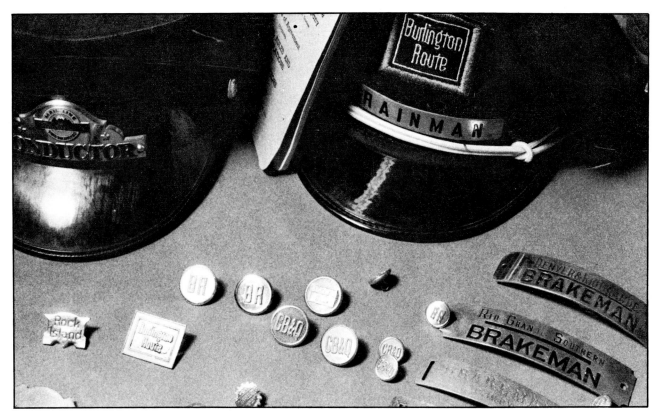

Rear: Railroad caps; $50–75 each. *Center:* Buttons; $3–9 ▲ each. *Right:* Cap badges; $15–25 each. *Left:* Lapel buttons; $8–15 each. All 1910–40. Relatively small and easily displayed, caps, buttons, and badges are among the top railroad collectibles. As in other areas, the older or more obscure the line to which it is related, the more desirable the button or badge.

Conductor's caps. *Left:* $45–60. *Right:* $60–75. Caps, like ▲ other uniform components, were purchased and owned by the railroadman. Since they seldom wore out on the job, quite a few have been preserved for posterity.

Enameled-brass and nickel-plate cap badges. *Left:* Santa Fe; 1940–50; $15–20. *Right:* Western trolley line; 1915–25; $20–25. Trainmen wore these badges on their caps to inform the public of their position and authority. When a cap wore out, badges could be removed and transferred to a new piece of headgear. ▲

Conductor's uniform in navy-blue wool; 1940–55; ▶
$125–160. The earliest American trainmen's uniforms were
patterned after English examples, and they have changed
very little over the years. Such clothing was not introduced
on U.S. lines until the late 19th century, in part because
workers resented having to buy clothing they could wear
only on the job.

▲
Railway workers' uniform buttons in brass and copper alloy;
1920–40; $15–20 each. Buttons were worn on coats, cuffs,
and to anchor cap bands. Smaller sizes, such as the Denver &
Rio Grande cap button *(lower left),* are regarded as the
most desirable.

Brass railroad locks; $12–15 each. Keys; $10–15 each. Key ▶
tags or tabs; $5–7 each. All 1900–40. Sturdy locks and
matching keys were essential to railroad security. The key
tags were surrendered by employees when checking out a
key and enabled the company to keep track of which keys
were in use.

Machinist's toolbox in pine, painted red and yellow with ▲ stenciled representation of early steam locomotive and tender; 1890–99; $250–300. This box was used in the Denver, Colo., shops of the Union Pacific, Denver & Gulf.

Unusually large (3' tall) crook-neck drinking-water can in ▲ aluminum; 1930–40; $30–40. Drinking water was essential to the crews maintaining the hot and dusty western rails. A young man, appropriately called a "water boy," was usually assigned the task of bringing refreshment to the section workers.

Early water pail of soldered and riveted tin; 1900–10; ▲ $35–50. The base of this pail is cone-shaped to make it useless on a hard, flat surface (like a kitchen table), thus reducing the likelihood that some employee would carry it off for use at home. It did, of course, serve quite adequately along the dirt right-of-way or as a fire pail.

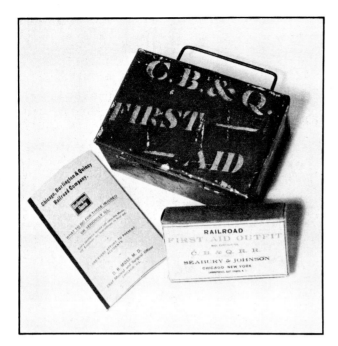

Wrecking car first-aid kit from one of the western narrow-gauge roads; 1900–20; $75–100. Wrecking cars were sent to the scene of an accident to aid the injured and to clear the rails. This box is sturdily made of wood and steel and is extremely rare.▼

First-aid kit in tin box, stenciled with initials of the Chicago, ▲ Burlington & Quincy; by Seabury & Johnson, Chicago, Ill.; 1910–25; $35–45. It is unusual to find an intact example of a first-aid kit, particularly one of this vintage.

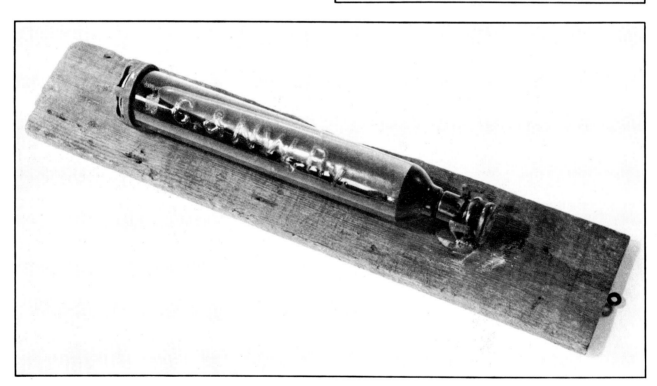

Elongated-glass fire extinguisher, embossed with the mark of ▲ the Colorado and North Western; 1900–10; $80–95. The tube contained fluid that produced a smothering foam when thrown on a fire. Although similar home fire extinguishers are quite common, few railroad extinguishers have survived.

Stencils in tin used in numbering railroad cars; 1920–40; ▲
$4–8 each. Freight cars, in particular, had their numbers
repainted frequently, depending on which line they were
operating and the goods they were carrying.

◄
Railroad spikes in wrought iron; 1920–40; $1–2 each.
Millions of ordinary spikes such as these exist (over 4 billion
are estimated to have been driven into U.S. ties over the
past century), making them among the least expensive of
all railroad collectibles.

Three examples of the Jeffery spike; $3–5 each. This unusual
spike was invented by Howard Greer of Chicago in 1888
and was used extensively on the Rio Grande Southern and
other western lines.
◄

Tool for determining track elevation in cast iron and wood, ▶
Silverton Northern; 1900–20; $80–100. Tools such as shovels,
pickaxes, and wrenches are common, but track gauges are
relatively hard to find.

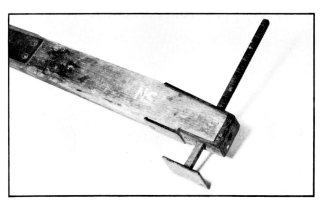

Reverse lever in cast and wrought iron, used in Denver & ▶
Royal Gorge engine of the K–37 class; 1903–15; $75–95.
These levers, also known as ''Johnson bars,'' were in use in
trains operating on the western narrow-gauge railroads.

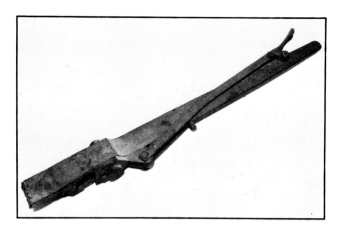

Keeley pump in red-painted tin; 1920–55; $125–165. Used ▲
to water-cool overheated gearboxes (hot boxes) on railroad
cars. The term *Keeley* is taken from the Keeley Institute
where so-called water cures were employed in the
treatment of alcoholism.

Railroad maintenance crew's gasoline-powered workcar; ▲ 1930–45; $1,500–2,000 restored. Vehicles like this replaced the old handcar as a means of moving track crews from place to place along the right-of-way.

◀

Water-hose carrier in cast iron and steel; 1900–20; $350–425. Carriers like this could be dragged about the railyards to wash down trains or, if necessary, to aid in putting out fires.

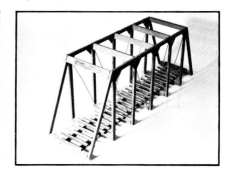

Model of wooden railroad bridge; ▲ 1920–25; $65–90. Some of the highest and longest wooden railway bridges were constructed in the western states, culminating in the building, in 1904, of a timber trestle for the Southern Pacific that extended 20 miles across the Great Salt Lake in Utah.

Chain-driven velocipede handcar; 1880–1900; $250–350. ▲ This bicyclelike conveyance was invented in 1879 by George Sheffield of Michigan. For a few years velocipedes were used by nonrailway personnel to travel up and down the rails. After several fatal accidents, their use was limited by law to railroad personnel.

Station Collectibles

The earliest railroads had no stations. Passengers arriving in a community ate and slept at the traditional taverns and inns that served stagecoach travelers. Tickets were sold on the trains or at designated locations. All this changed with the westward expansion of the rail lines. On the Great Plains and in the mountains there were few inns; indeed, for the most part there were no towns. As the rails advanced, the companies found it necessary to establish fueling and watering stops every ten miles or so, and ''tank towns'' (so-called for the tall water tanks that graced their skylines) sprang up around these stops. Stations were built, and they grew with the new communities.

Collectibles associated with railway stations are many and varied. Ticket booths, benches, handcarts, lighting fixtures, and a variety of different signs may be found. For the true railroad buff ticket booths or waiting-room benches have historic importance, and he or she seeks them out for their association either with railroading in general or with a specific line. With furnishings, however, there is competition from noncollectors who view the massive benches and cabinets as attractive additions to their homes.

Some signs have appeal for more than just railroad aficionados, for collectors of advertising antiques (or ''advertiques,'' as they are known in the trade) eagerly seek railway travel posters. On the other hand, such collectors have little interest in station and right-of-way signs, so large numbers of these important mementos of railroading's past remain available to the seeker of railway memorabilia.

Other more mundane collectibles include the spittoons once so common in every station and the portable steps that enabled passengers to reach the high thresholds of early passenger trains. Both these items were frequently marked by the railroad that owned them, a factor that substantially enhances their value.

Cast-iron, steel, and glass fare ▲ box; by Johnson Manufacturing Co.; patented 1914; $450–550. Though also used in trains, fare boxes of this sort were most often used in trolley cars. Examples in working order are favorites with railroad buffs.

Reconstruction of railroad ticket ▶ office cage; 1900–10. Enclosure; $1,600–2,200. Hanging kerosene lamp; $90–115. Santa Fe advertising sign; $85–115. As the railroads built their way west, they opened small stations furnished in this manner at each community along the line.

Cast-iron and oak ▲ waiting-room bench; 1910–25; $250–300. Benches such as this were a common sight in many railroad stations until the end of World War II. Today, they are enjoying a rebirth as dining-room or patio furniture.

Front: Colorado & Southern cast iron and oak baggage-handler's barrow; 1920–30; $75–90. Leather-covered railway trunk; 1890–1910; $35–45. *Rear:* Solid-oak waiting-room bench, 12' long; 1920–30; $400–500. ◄

Oak and cast-iron baggage cart; 1880–1900; $325–375. ▲
Baggage carts were once a common sight at all western
railroad terminals. The simple iron wheels mark this as an
earlier example. The sheet-steel milk cans were used to ship
milk to market. Today, they are collectors' items at $20–35
each.

Sheet-steel and cast-iron railway station sign; New Mexico; ▶
1925–35; $115–145. This tan-and-orange sign could be
picked up and moved from place to place as required.
Other train-berth signs were hung on walls or sign racks. They
represent an important area of railroad memorabilia.

Railway Express Agency sign in sheet ▲
steel, lithographed in yellow and
black; 1930–50; $275–350. This sign is
over 6' long and was hung on the
exterior wall of the agency building.

Speed-limit sign in ▲
sheet steel, stenciled
black on white;
1930–40; $65–80.
This sign, placed at
the entrance to the
railroad yard,
advised engineers
that both passenger
and freight trains
were limited to a
speed of no more
than 10 miles per
hour.

Railway sign in sheet steel, stenciled black on white; ▲
1940–50; $120–150. This sign once marked Biggs Spur, a
branch line north of Chama, N.Mex., which was discontinued
and torn up in 1951.

Lithographed tin railway signs. *Above* and *Center:* Signs for men's and women's restrooms used in both trains and stations; 1940–60; $20–30 each. *Below:* Builder's sign used on railway cars constructed by the Pullman Co., Pullman, Ill.; 1940–55; $30–35.
◄

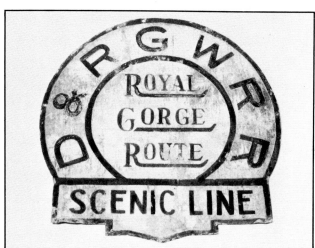

Denver & Rio Grande Western railroad sign in sheet steel, ▶ lithographed black on white; 1926–36; $145–185. This sign, which could have been used in a station or on the train itself, advertised the famous Royal Gorge route, a scenic area of the Rockies where narrow-gauge trains passed through a gorge more than a thousand feet deep.

Missouri Pacific ▶ lithographed-tin perpetual calendar; 1935–45; $125–150. Advertising calendars are among the most popular of railroad advertising memorabilia; when in good condition they always bring high prices.

Colorado Midland railway advertising poster, lithographed in red, white, green, and black; 1915; $375–450. This spectacular poster promoted the last grand council of North American Indians, but was clearly designed to attract railway tourists, not Indians. It represents the very best graphically in railway advertising. ◄

Rio Grande lithographed-paper advertising sign; 1950–60; ► $55–70. This rather late poster also advertised the scenic wonders of the Royal Gorge.

Western Pacific tourist brochure of lithographed ▲
paper; 1900–15; $25–35. Since an influx of settlers was
crucial to the western roads in order that they might have
passengers and freight as well as sell their government land
grants, the lines began early to issue promotional
materials. As the number of settlers waned, promotions
turned to tourism.

Denver & Rio Grande step box used to reduce the distance ▲
between train step and station platform, wood; 1920–30;
$25–35.

◄

Early cast-iron cuspidor; 1880–1910; $60–70. Until well into
the 20th century, a large number of men used chewing
tobacco, necessitating cuspidors in all public facilities,
including railroad trains and stations.

Collectibles from the Dining Car

Before the introduction of the first dining car, in 1868, railroad passengers ate on the run and under rather unappealing conditions. However, with the popularization of in-train dining, luxury became the byword. Lines vied with each other to provide the finest service and the most elegant silver, crystal, and china. Menus as varied as those in major restaurants were offered, and some lines, such as the Santa Fe, even served dishes appropriate to the regions through which they passed.

By the early 1870s travelers on nearly all the eastern railways were served in dining cars, but things moved more slowly in the West. In 1876 Fred Harvey opened the first modern (for its day) depot restaurant in the Atchison, Topeka & Santa Fe station at Topeka, Kansas. Buoyed by that success, Harvey then induced the Santa Fe to build more such facilities and, by 1900, to include dining cars on its passenger trains. This innovation was soon copied by other western lines, but because of this late start most western dining-car items are post-1900.

Electroplated silver was widely used on all railroads, and most examples found bear a railway monogram or name. It is thus possible to assemble complete sets not only of flatware but of serving dishes such as coffeepots, gravy boats, and hot plates as well. Much of this silver is Art Deco in design, reflecting its use on the great streamliners of the 1930s. The marks of some of America's best-known silver manufacturers, such as Reed & Barton and Gorham, will be found on railway plate. Though increasing in popularity among collectors, silver is still available in some quantity and is reasonably priced.

Crystal and ordinary glass were used extensively on the western lines, but they were frequently unmarked, probably because of cost and high breakage. However, it is possible to obtain monogrammed water carafes, pitchers, and even glasses. Finer crystal was usually reserved for specialty items such as centerpieces and candelabra.

Most abundant and most sought after by railroad enthusiasts is railway china, which is seldom true china or porcelain but rather ironstone, a form of white earthenware durable enough to survive dining-room use. This ware was made by many well-known early-twentieth-century American potteries, including Homer Laughlin, Syracuse China, and Hall Brothers.

Art Deco crystal whale; 1930–40; $150–200. Used as a decorative centerpiece in dining ▲ cars of the Central Pacific, this sophisticated piece is both etched and cut and represents the best in railway glass.

Set of electroplated silver, Western Pacific; 1935–40; ▲ $75–95. By combining various interchangeable and multipurpose elements of this set, railway personnel could produce saucers, sherbets, glass holders, and other pieces.

Electroplated covered serving dish, Western Pacific; ▲ 1930–40; $80–100. Although most railway serving dishes were of plate, some lines used base metal such as nickel silver or pewter. Whatever the material, rough, constant use made quality a must for such ware.

Electroplated silver: 1920–35. *Bottom:* Platter, Missouri ▲ Pacific; $40–45. *On plate:* Table crumber, Milwaukee; $25–30. *Right:* Covered sugar bowl, stamped PULLMAN and probably used on Pullman Co.-leased dining cars; $35–45.

Ironstone china, marked with logo of Union Pacific; 1935–45. *Left:* Bread-and-butter plate; $11–15. *Center top:* Dessert bowl; $15–19. *Center bottom:* Dinner plate; $25–28. *Right:* Demitasse cup and saucer; $22–26. ◀

Ironstone ``States'' plate, Missouri Pacific; 1935–40; $160–210. This plate's high price is justified because it bears a representation of a train and because it is part of a limited issue commemorating the states through which the Missouri Pacific operated during the 1930s. ▼

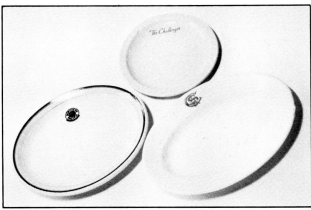

Ironstone platters. *Left:* Northern Pacific; 1930–40; $48–55. ▲ *Center:* The Challenger, Union Pacific; 1940–55; $17–20. *Right:* Colorado & Southern; 1890–95; $400–500. The very high price for the C&S platter reflects the fact that it is one of only a very few surviving examples from one of the West's first dining cars.

Extremely rare historical platter, Union Pacific; 1890–1900; $550–600. This unique platter is decorated with lithographed depictions of life in the Old West: a bison, Pony Express rider, stagecoach, and so forth. It is one of the very few pre-1900 western railway commemoratives. ◀

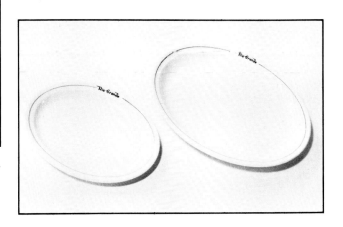

Ironstone platters, Rio Grande; 1935–45; $18–27. Platters ▶ such as these are easily obtained and can form the basis for a growing collection.

The western lines all produced attractive dining-car china patterns, and it is possible, as with silver, to obtain sets of related pieces ranging into the dozens. Some collectors, though, seek out at least a single example from every line or concentrate on a particular type such as coffee cups or bread plates. Pattern is important, and ware depicting trains or western scenery is particularly in demand, but rarity is of even greater importance. China used on short-lived lines or issued in small quantities to commemorate a special occasion is in greatest demand and, consequently, most costly. On the other hand, the many railroad dispersal sales of the 1960s have placed large quantities of common dining-room china on the market, and this ware remains inexpensive.

The marking or monogramming of dining-room ware not only reduced the chances of theft but also afforded yet another way of promoting railways. Many lines carried this concept further by offering their passengers everything from ashtrays to paperweights, all suitably emblazoned with the name of the line on which they were traveling. These items also present an interesting field for the collector.

Communications Devices

The vast distances and frowning mountain ranges of the western United States presented the railroads with many problems, not least among them communication. Fortunately, though, by the time the lines began to stretch west from the Mississippi that problem had been largely solved by the introduction of the telegraph as a means of communication between trains and stations. A transcontinental telegraph line was established in 1861, eight years before the rail linkage was achieved, and it was a simple matter to ally the rails with the lines.

The value of such an association had been proved years before. As early as 1851 dispatchers began to replace handwritten and hand-delivered orders with faster telegraphic instructions, and the introduction of high-speed Morse systems during the 1880s assured the supremacy of this method until it was replaced by the telephone during the 1920s.

Though in service for many long years, the railway telegraph system has left us few mementos. Transmitters, receivers, and related amplification devices are in some demand, but those that can be shown to have been used on the railroads are but a fraction of all such devices. Much more common and of great interest to some collectors are the insulators used to shield the live lines from the poles on which they were strung. Some of these cone- or umbrella-shaped devices are made of pottery and a few early wooden examples are known, but the vast majority are of clear or blue-green glass.

The first of such insulators were threadless and simply fit over a peg on the telegraph pole, but a more securely locking threaded type was invented in 1865, and these were employed on the western lines. Many insulators bear an embossed manufacturer's mark, and names such as Brookfield, Hemingray, and Whitall-Tatum are frequently seen. As a group, insulators are quite inexpensive, costing but a few dollars each. Threadless ones, though, and those in unusual colors such as cobalt blue or amber will bring prices in the hundreds of dollars.

Though the telegraph served its purpose well, railwaymen were quick to see the advantages inherent in the telephone—more rapid transmission, universal communication with a nontelegraphic world, and less need for trained personnel. Consequently, railway lines began installing telephones as soon as they were perfected and became available in quantity. By the 1920s most lines had converted completely. While switchboards, carrying boxes, and early repair equipment are of interest, most collectors seek out the telephones themselves. Most favored are the attractive brass units used in stations and offices. These are now being converted for use in modern homes and offices. Also collectible are the black Bakelite "candlestick" phones and the unusual "scissors-type" wall units that were used by railway dispatchers.

Abandoned telegraph poles, southern Wyoming. When the first transcontinental telegraph line was completed on October 22, 1861, it revolutionized American communications, particularly as related to the railroads. Telegraph had been used as early as 1851 to regulate the movement of trains, and once the western line was up it was utilized extensively by the advancing rail lines.

Telegraph line insulator in deep-green glass; by Hemingray Co.; 1900–10; $12–15. This insulator is made by one of the major producers. Rarer examples may sell for several hundred dollars each.

Telegraph line insulators; 1920–35; $6–9 each. Insulators ▲ range in size from 2″ tall to over 6″ and in color from clear glass through shades of blue and green into unusual hues like red and purple. They are avidly collected by specialists in the field, as well as by bottle collectors.

Railway telegraph keys; 1900–20. *Left:* $35–40. *Right:* $50–60. Until replaced by telephones in the 1930s, the telegraph was central to the running and organization of American railways. ◀

Expandable wall telephone; by Western Electric; 1920–30; $80–100. The telescoping carriage of this dispatcher's telephone allows the dispatcher greater freedom. ▼

Brass and Bakelite depot telephone, Rio Grande; 1923; $195–245. The introduction of the telephone to the railroads proved to be a real boon to management. Not only did it allow for faster communication, but it also eliminated the need for trained and therefore higher-paid telegraphers. ◀

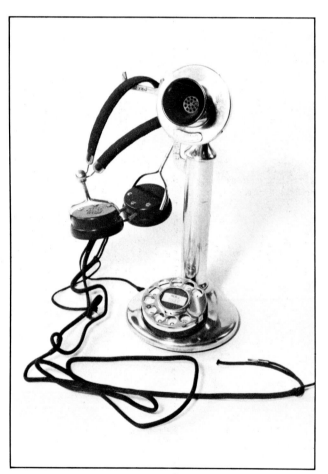

◀

Leather carrying box for portable telephone, Denver & Rio Grande Western; 1925–35; $65–80. Portable telephones were used by work crews and other isolated railway personnel.

Wooden trolley-car telephone box; 1920–30; $75–100. Telephones were placed in boxes like this along a trolley line so that motormen could report their positions to the central dispatcher.

◀

REPORT

7.

They Plowed the Plains

In many respects the settling of the West was the American dream brought to realization. The East had been crowded for many generations, its economics and politics controlled by a wealthy elite. Contrary to popular fiction, in most cases the poor stayed poor, subsisting on tiny, unproductive hill farms or struggling in big-city slums. For them, the seemingly endless prairies offered an opportunity almost beyond imagining.

Like many dreams, this one was part nightmare. Much of the western legend was a lie fostered by railroads eager to sell off land grants and by speculators hoping to reap fortunes by disposing of almost worthless desert. Since most of the prospective settlers had never seen the lands they were being enticed to buy, it was surprisingly easy to convince them, for example, that the Dakota badlands were "a paradise where mockingbirds and paraquets [sic] and cockatoos warble musical challenges to each other amid the rich foliage of the sweet bay and mango trees."

In a day when caveat emptor was the byword, such fabrications were regarded as just "good business." But there was an element of truth in all the advertising. The West, particularly the coastal states and Texas, was immensely rich. But as the migrants soon found out, much of this bounty could be realized only through methods beyond their means.

The migrants were a diverse group. From the rich but crowded Mississippi valley came seasoned farmers, often well to do and inured to hardship. From the South there were newly liberated blacks who by 1870 were farming over twenty thousand acres in Kansas alone. There were the Irish who populated the Dakota Territory, the Scandinavians and the Germans who planted a little bit of Pennsylvania in the Texas hill country. All hurried to grab their piece of the dream.

The first settlers traveled by Conestoga wagon, the sturdy vehicle that came to symbolize the westward movement. Hopeful settlers would assemble in one of the trans-Mississippi frontier towns like Tipton, Missouri, in the springtime. Once the grass was high enough for grazing and the ground firm underfoot, they would start out. Most wagon trains were made up of twenty-five or thirty wagons under the command of an experienced wagon master and guide. The trip would take months, and there would be little chance to gather provisions along the way, so the Conestogas would be laden with barrels of flour and hundreds of pounds of ham, sugar,

salt, coffee, and dried beans. Hardly a varied menu, but, hopefully, one that would suffice.

In the beginning the wagon trains traveled to California and Oregon, even though it was a two-thousand-mile trip. This area was rich and relatively safe. Until the late 1870s the prairies, by comparison, were the home of Indians whose attitude toward the intruders was understandably unfriendly.

The trip west by wagon was never easy. The trails were bare traces winding through alkaline flats, red-man-infested forests, and almost impassable mountains. Rivers, like the great Columbia, barred the way, forcing the settlers to set their wagons on rafts and float them across perilous rapids. These were, perhaps, the lesser evils. Far more migrants died of disease than succumbed to accident or Indian attack. As early as 1849 cholera struck voyagers on the California-Oregon trail; and smallpox, typhoid, malaria, and a host of children's ailments helped to fill the unmarked graves that stood like dismal signposts along the way.

Many travelers were unprepared for these hardships. Ill advised or deliberately misled, they started out driving herds of eastern cattle accustomed to the lush grass of the Berkshires; even their traveling clothing was frequently more suitable to a Boston wedding than a Utah campfire. The trail took its toll in human lives, in the clumps of dead cattle along the trail, and in the pathetic heaps of belongings abandoned by people who found that their starving oxen could no longer pull their overloaded wagons.

Still they pressed on, and during the 1860s their numbers increased sharply. The first cause for this was the Homestead Act of 1862, which provided that any person above the age of twenty-one could obtain free title to a quarter section (160 acres) of public land by paying a registration fee of ten dollars, residing on his or her claim for five consecutive years, and "improving" it. The latter requirement was always generously construed and usually satisfied by building a house.

For the dirt-poor hill farmer and the landless artisan this offer must have seemed like a gate to heaven. The key was provided in 1869 with the opening of the first transcontinental railway. The expanding western lines needed passengers as well as farmers to buy their grant lands and to use their shipping facilities. They went after these potential customers in a most aggressive way, offering special low rates on "immigrant trains" and

Preceding pages: Woodenware; 1890–1910. *Left*: Oblong chopping bowl; $70–85. *Center top*: Covered sugar bucket; $35–45. *Center bottom*: Chopper; $18–25. *Right*: Potato masher; $8–11. Many early settlers used wooden utensils extensively, but, contrary to popular opinion, most of these objects—like the ones shown here—were made in eastern factories.

advertising the wonders of the West, "where every man can become a millionaire."

The immigrant coaches had hard seats and often lacked heat in winter, but they were faster, safer, and more comfortable than the prairie schooner. Settlers didn't abandon the Conestoga entirely, but after 1870 more and more took to the rails for their trip west.

The previous trickle became a flood. Between 1863 and 1890 nearly one million homestead applications were filed. When one adds to this the thousands who bought their land from private parties, the magnitude of the movement becomes evident.

But the figures can be deceptive. Scholars reckon that only one of every nine homestead applications was genuine. Most reflected various devices employed by speculators to get their hands on public property. In the Southwest, for example, ranch owners would send their employees out to file claims and then buy them out for a few dollars or a bottle of whiskey. False affidavits for improvements on homestead tracts were commonplace but seldom detected, for on-site inspections were not possible with the land so vast and inspectors so few.

Still, there were many legitimate homesteaders. They fought their way, against odds, across the mountains and the desert and staked out their claims. In the North they built pole cabins of rough-hewn logs, chinked with mud and heated by stone fireplaces. On the treeless plains they lived in dugouts cut into the earth or in homes made of sod, the "Kansas brick," which was sliced into oblong sections and stacked like today's cement blocks. Both types of dwellings had advantages. They were reasonably warm, and they didn't blow down in the howling prairie windstorms. They also had disadvantages. When it rained, the sod or buffalo-grass roofs leaked so badly that the woman of the house often held an umbrella over her head while cooking. Dirt from the walls kept the interior filthy, and every imaginable form of wildlife, including rattlesnakes, sheltered in the loamy walls.

Housing was only one of the settlers' worries. The land presented problems never encountered in the eastern United States. It was rich, treeless, and rockless, but in many areas it was also too arid to farm in the conventional manner. The prairie topsoil was covered by a foot-thick mat of grass that defied plows. When this vegetation was removed, the constant winds blew away the dry loam. To the threat of dust storms was added that of prairie fires that could scorch thousands of acres and bring death to livestock. Sub-zero weather was common during the winter, and raging blizzards might isolate a family for days.

If one did succeed in raising a crop amid all this, there were also insect pests to contend with—swarms of grasshoppers appeared each summer, eating everything in sight, including window curtains and leather harnesses.

But the hardiest and the smartest hung on. They worked together to raise houses and barns with the new lumber brought west on the railway flatcars. They learned to cope with the environment. If there was available surface water, they irrigated and found that one acre of such watered land could produce as much as ten acres had in the East.

Where there were no streams and not enough annual rainfall, the farmers drilled wells. In river valleys and a few similar places where the water table approached the surface, wells could be dug by hand as they had been back home, but in most plains states shafts had to be driven down hundreds of feet, and windmills were required to raise the water.

Technology came to the aid of the less fortunate. The technique of "dry farming," long known in the Near East, could be utilized to raise crops in all but the most arid years. Moreover, new machinery, available on time payments, was designed to meet the problems presented by the western soil and climate. Fine steel plows had replaced the earlier iron-sheathed wooden ones soon after the Civil War, and during the 1870s improved harrows, seeders, and threshers appeared. These big machines were designed to work large expanses of land—the migrants had discovered that even 160 acres were not enough, because hundreds of acres were required for dry farming. Those who could not afford the necessary equipment or survive the bad years sold out, and the abandoned farms were bought up or were turned back to their former use as grazing land.

Though there were panics and "hard times," progress was on the side of the western farmers. All through the second half of the nineteenth century the cities of the Midwest and East continued to grow. Their burgeoning industries needed workers, and the workers needed food—too much food to ever be supplied by local agriculture. Again the railroads had the answer. They shipped the beef cattle driven to Kansas railheads and the wheat that could be found in silos along the right-of-way from Oklahoma to North Dakota.

Today when one travels through the West it is difficult to imagine what it must have seemed like to the settlers who came there in the nineteenth century, but a portion of their stubborn, resilient character remains in those who farm there, and the land remains, too, as vast and difficult and promising as it ever was.

Transportation Collectibles

Travel in the West was always difficult. In some areas lack of water was a problem; in others there was too much water or high mountains barred the way. But even where these impediments did not exist, there was the problem of distance. It was over two thousand miles from St. Louis to San Francisco, and any homesteader going west had to anticipate a journey of many hundreds of miles.

How to get there? For the early explorers it had often been "shank's mare," and more than one adventurer had walked all the way to the coast. For most, though, there was the horse, the mule, or the burro, and some form of wheeled conveyance. In the Southwest this was the *carreta*, a crude wood-wheeled cart. Up North a similar vehicle, called the pembina buggy, hauled skins from Canada's Red River valley to St. Paul, Minnesota. These wagons were slow, lacked springs, and their ungreased wheels emitted an ear-piercing screech.

There had to be a better way, and it appeared during the 1830s in the form of the Conestoga wagon. Developed in Pennsylvania (it is named for a Pennsylvania town), the Conestoga was originally a freight carrier, built for use in the Appalachians. Its out-turned saucer-shaped wheels were designed for control and steering ease on mountain roads, and its boat-shaped body prevented cargo from shifting on steep grades. A stout canvas top protected the contents from inclement weather.

The Conestoga was big. Drawn by two to four oxen, it could carry up to three thousand pounds. Small wonder, then, that by 1840 most travelers setting out for the plains employed this form of transportation. As the great canvas-covered wagons bobbed across the rolling prairies, they looked a bit like boats under sail—hence the well-known term "prairie schooner."

When they finally got where they were going, the settlers didn't abandon their Conestogas. The big wagons could serve as farm or market vehicles, and, in a pinch, as shelter until a house was put up. But they were slow and much too large for most purposes. Every householder looked forward to the day when he could afford a buckboard or, perhaps, one of those fancy buggies made in the eastern factories.

Even during the early days there had been faster transportation. Stagecoaches had operated regularly in New England since the 1700s, and as far back as 1850 there had been a monthly coach between Indepen-dence, Missouri, and Santa Fe, New Mexico. The vehicle used was the Concord, a four- to six-horse coach with an egg-shaped body hung on leather braces strung between its axles. Because of this construction the Concord had a rolling motion rather than the usual jolting one. It couldn't accommodate many passengers—perhaps six on the two padded interior seats and another one or two on the driver's platform—but it made good time, as much as five miles per hour if the road was decent.

Concords carried the mail, passengers prosperous enough to afford the substantial fares, and the Wells Fargo strongbox, a repository of wealth that all too often attracted the attention of local bad men.

A fair number of Conestoga wagons and Concord coaches have survived in museums and private collections, but they can hardly be regarded as common. Various accessories used on such vehicles are available, however, and collectors seek out things like Conestoga toolboxes (with their elaborate wrought-iron decoration), water barrels, metal fixtures, coach lights, and painted door panels. All tell the story of western transportation before it came to be dominated by the train and the motorcar.

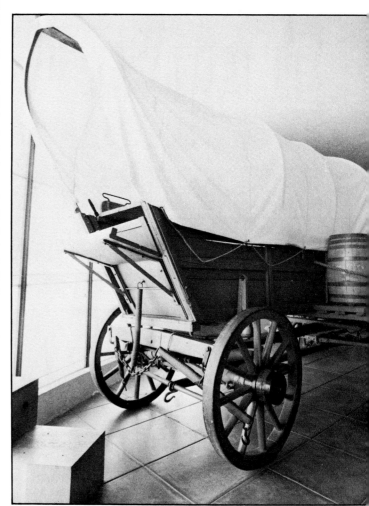

Conestoga wagon; 1850–70; $3,000–3,750. Sturdy and ▶ capacious, the Conestoga was the dominant vehicle on the Santa Fe Trail from 1830 to 1850 and also carried thousands of settlers to California and Oregon.

Detail of suspension system on the Conestoga wagon. Built to last, the sturdy Conestogas endured everything from rocky and rutted trails to great rivers— down which they were poled like rafts. ▼

Concord stagecoach used on the Mendocino, Calif., line; ▲ 1850–60; $4,500–5,500. Repainted in its original maroon and white, this Concord is typical of hundreds made in Massachusetts and used in the Far West.

Dome-top traveling case covered in leather and decorated with brass studs; 1840–60; $90–115. The earliest settlers used boxes like this to carry valuables and small items. ◄

Coach lamp in brass and painted tin ▲ with whale-oil burner; 1840–50; $250–300. Coach lamps are in great demand not only by collectors but by decorators.

Late Victorian suitcases. *Above:* Pressed tin grained to resemble alligator; 1880–95; $75–100. *Below:* Cardboard; 1920–30; $20–30. Once weight became a factor in the cost of transporting luggage, a wide range of lightweight materials was pressed into service in the luggage industry. ◄

Farm Implements

To the farmer, the western prairies must have seemed like heaven on earth. Covered with shoulder-high buffalo grass and usually free of rocks or trees, they stood in sharp contrast to the thin-soiled rockbound hills of New England. The climate was generally milder, too. In the Southwest and in California winters were so mild that stock barns were not required, and even farther north wheat grew like weeds in the deep and fertile topsoil.

By the time the westward movement began in earnest, around 1850, farming technology was sufficiently advanced to allow exploitation of these riches. The agriculturists came equipped with some knowledge of irrigation and drainage and with tools that had not existed a few decades earlier.

Nearly every wagon carried a plow—a good, iron, factory-made one rather than the crude, wooden affairs employed by the *campesinos* in New Mexico. Tin-and-metal corn and potato planters were used, as were patent corn huskers and produce sorters. There was still plenty of back-breaking stoop labor, but the new inventions greatly facilitated the planting and harvesting of the western farmsteads, which were measured in hundreds of acres rather than dozens—as had been the case "back East."

Since there were few factories west of St. Louis, nearly all this equipment was made in the East and shipped to the West. That makes it no less collectible, however, as long as it saw service on the plains.

There were many homemade tools as well, some that had remained unchanged for hundreds of years. Until the coming of horse-drawn or steam-driven harvesters, most hay had to be cut by hand with the picturesque but man-killing scythe. Hay was then thrown into wagons with an iron pitchfork and, later, cut into usable portions with an odd-looking hay knife. Rakes, hoes, and shovels (including all-wood ones) were also still very much in evidence.

Nor was there much change in the way animals were used and cared for. Oxen, which did much of the heavy work around the farm, were shod with wrought iron by the local farrier or smithy and harnessed in large, handmade wooden yokes. A harness maker provided gear for the resident mules and horses. Cows were milked by hand, and the pails were carried to and from the barn on a wooden shoulder yoke.

Had these technical factors been all that the homesteader had to contend with, the West would truly have been a paradise. Unfortunately, there were other problems. Fencing is vital to farming because animals, both wild and domestic, cannot be allowed into the fields. But fencing presented both practical and political dilemmas. On the one hand, wooden fencing was practically unobtainable on the almost treeless plains. Where posts could be had, either through importation or through use of stone, it was soon discovered that buffalo and wild cattle had little regard for the woven wire brought from the East.

In 1867 Lucien Smith offered a solution to this problem when he patented the first barbed wire. This was made of a strand of wire on which were suspended wooden blocks pierced with sharp nails. The idea didn't prove practical, however, nor did several later types, such as the spurlike rowels used in Hunt's Patent and the sawtooth ribbon wire known as Buckthorn. However, when Joseph Glidden invented a simple, pronged, double-strand wire in 1876, the solution was found.

But new obstacles arose as the farmers (and some large landholders) began to fence their acres. Sheep owners and cattlemen, accustomed to raising their stock on public lands, saw their grazing and water rights cut off. They rebelled and began to cut fences, burn barns, and destroy crops. In the most violent upheavals, such as the Texas "Fence-cutter's War" of 1893, stock and men died. It was nearly a decade before all rights were resolved and the farmers could feel secure.

The farmer had other problems as well. In many areas drought was a constant threat, warded against by use of storage tanks and deep, windmill-powered wells. There were dust storms, too, once the protective grass and topsoil had been removed. And in forest areas, there was the fear of fire. If one adds to these the fear of Indians and outlaws, it is apparent that the farmers' "winning of the West" was indeed a heroic achievement.

▲

Plow in steel and cast iron; 1870–90; $135–155. Many of the pioneer wagons crossing the western plains carried a small plow to be used in breaking ground for the first crops.

◄

Corn planter in iron and tin; 1890–1920; $30–40. Efficient tools such as this greatly reduced the amount of stoop labor involved in farming and facilitated planting of the greater acreage common in the West.

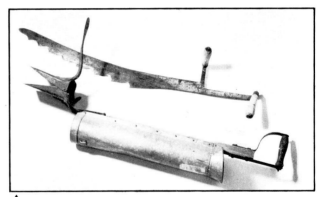

▲

Above: Hay knife in iron; 1900–10; $35–45. This sawlike tool was used to cut apart bales of hay used for animal fodder. *Below:* Potato planter in iron and tin; 1910–25; $35–45. Seed potatoes stored in the tin sleeve slid down into the iron jaws where they could be forced into the soil and released by pressure on the foot pedal.

Machine for sharpening sickles and scythes; 1890–1910; $75–90. This interesting hand-operated sharpener was probably used on a large stock farm where many edged tools would be in use.

◄

Open-pit saw in iron
and wood;
1870–80; $110–130.
In those areas of the
West where wood
was available,
planks were cut out
with a pit saw
wielded by two
men, one of whom
stood on a trestle
while the other
handled the saw
from below. ▶

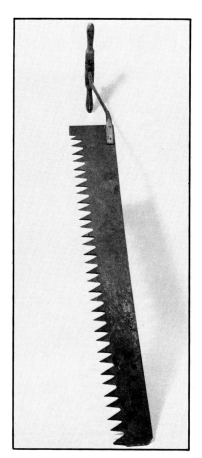

Grain or apple shovel in wood; 1880–1900; $90–115. ▲
Wooden shovels were used with grain to avoid the sparks
caused by the contact of steel on stone, which could ignite
the combustible grain dust. They were also preferred with
apples because they lessened bruising of the fruit.

◀

Left and *Right:* Forks used in harvesting potatoes; 1900–20;
$25–32. *Center:* Large coal-handling fork of the sort used
when coal heating became common on the plains;
1900–20; $40–50. A variety of forks were used on the
western farm.

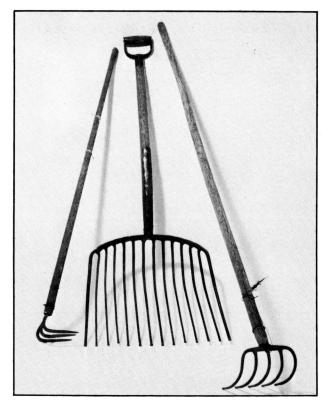

Early barbed wire on a crude, rough-hewn fence post in ▲
Colorado. Farmers often used fresh-cut saplings or dead tree
trunks for fence posts because they were cheap and readily
available.

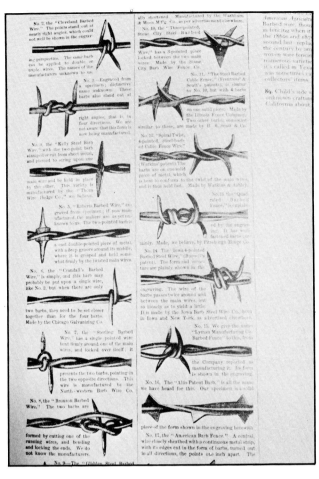

Illustration from early farm magazine indicating the various types of patent barbed wire available during the late 19th century. Wire of this sort may range in price from as little as $5 to as much as $100 for the standard 12"-to-18" sample. ◄

Ox shoes of wrought iron; 1890–1900; $7–11. The unusual shape of the shoe was dictated by the nature of the beast's hoof and the work it was expected to do. ▼

Ox yoke in wood; 1870–80; $140–185. Oxen are powerful creatures, and massive oaken yokes as much as 4' long were used to control them. Today these yokes are extremely popular as mantel decorations and lighting fixtures. Double yokes such as this are more common than ◄ single ones.

Above: Pair of hames; $17–26. *Below:* Single- or whiffletree; $13–18. Both 1900–10. Local harness makers and smithies made some horse tack, but the majority was bought from large eastern manufacturers. Sears Roebuck catalogs of the early 20th century advertised a wide variety of harness- and draft-horse equipment. ▼

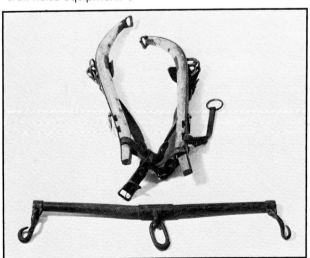

The early furnishings of western homes were crudely made and few in number. A "prairie schooner" could carry only the barest of necessities: trunks, a few chairs tied on behind, and, perhaps, a favorite cupboard. All else had to be manufactured or purchased once the "promised land" was reached. Consequently, authenticated pre-1870 western furniture is confined primarily to basics: chairs, benches, beds, and storage chests.

Once the railroads were in operation, however, a veritable flood of eastern factory-made furniture—products of the enormous shops at places like Grand Rapids, Michigan—began to pour into the plains states. Small, local manufacturers such as those that had existed in New England seldom had a chance to get going, and the great bulk of collectible western furniture is actually eastern in origin.

A similar situation existed with other household goods. Most travelers carried tinware to cook in and eat from because it was both lightweight and sturdy. No doubt there were a few barrels of precious porcelain or "china" ware in some wagons, too, but more than one household had to get by for months or even years on housewares of tin and home-carved wood. The railroads solved that problem, too. It wasn't long before common yellowware bowls from the potteries at Liverpool, Ohio, and Trenton, New Jersey, and imported English white ironstone were available from prairie storekeepers—at an appropriate premium, of course.

Lighting was a problem because the settlers were a long way from the gaslights and whale-oil lamps of the eastern seaboard. But they did have buffalo and cattle, and tallow candles could be made from their fat. During the 1880s kerosene became available, and the kerosene lamp became the standard lighting device in western homes. Heat, which could be provided by a fire of buffalo chips or compressed straw, could also be obtained with kerosene, so the clear fluid assumed an unusual importance on the treeless plains.

Much of what the settlers used had to be brought from the East, but much was also made at home. The cows and goats gave milk that could be drunk or made into butter and cheese. The first churns were fashioned locally, but patented factory versions were soon available. Butter molds were bought or carved at home while sitting before the fire on a winter night. Such homely items as rolling pins, vegetable scrapers, and mixing bowls could also be shaped from available timber scraps.

Naturally, the farm wife hoped for something a bit better. She might start out washing the family clothing in a nearby stream, but she would soon graduate to an oak tub and a patent washboard, and, hopefully, from these to one of the crude, hand-powered washing machines that were developed in the late nineteenth century. Like most farm chores, doing the laundry wasn't fun, but the new equipment reduced the drudgery.

The women, like their menfolk, brought west with them the skills they had learned at home. They took scraps of worn-out clothing and made gay quilts for the beds or sturdy rag rugs for the floor. Where they could get or make woolen yarn, they fashioned Berlin-work wall plaques with mottoes such as "Home Sweet Home" to brighten the walls of the cabin or sod house. They baked cookies, cutting them out with a tin cutter. And, of course, they canned. Development of the airtight glass canning jar in 1858 revolutionized food preservation. With a safe and easy way to "put by" vegetables and meats, the rural families found themselves for the first time able to survive the dreaded bad year. Unfortunately, however, these same families could not survive the changes in the economy that have gradually made the family farm obsolete and have turned to dust the dream of the western voyagers.

Chopping bowls in wood turned on a lathe; 1900–20; ▲ $16–36. Similar bowls were still being advertised in Sears Roebuck catalogs during the 1920s. They were used for everything from eating to food preparation.

Vegetable scrapers in wood; 1890–1915. *Left:* Slaw cutter; $23–32. *Center:* Vegetable scraper; $14–18. *Right:* Patent slaw cutter; $30–40. All these utensils are factory made; the patent slaw cutter bears the label of a Kansas City manufacturer. ▼

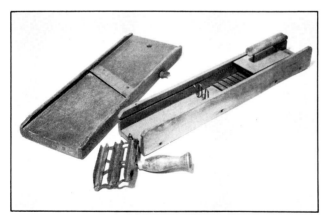

Cake or cookie ▶ mold in hand-carved walnut; 1870–80; $145–165. The Germanic settlers of Texas brought with them the so-called springerle molds used in baking in both Germany and Pennsylvania.

Detail of chopping bowl showing repair made by a thrifty ▲ householder; Denver, Colo.; 1870–80; $65–75. Rather than decreasing value, an unusual and early repair such as this enhances it. This bowl was turned on a crude home lathe.

Bale-handle storage box in wood with matching cover; ▲ 1880–1900; $45–60. Boxes like this had many uses. Some were employed in taking cheese or butter to market, and others contained spices or herbs.

Miniature dome-top box painted in salmon and pale green; northern plains; 1870–90; $225–275. This receptacle was probably brought west by European immigrants. ▲

Tinware; 1880–1910. *Left:* Cake mold; $13–17. *Center left:* Scoop; $10–15. *Center right:* Milk can; $25–35. *Right:* Funnel; $7–9. During the second half of the 19th century, western settlers used large quantities of factory-made tinware because it was both light and durable. ▼

Cookie molds in tin; 1890–1900; $11–17 each. Fanciful ▲ molds and the cookies they produced added a festive note to the often somber prairie home. Collectors look for larger examples and those featuring unusual creatures such as lions, elephants, and ostriches.

Left: Cigar case in tin; $9–13. *Center:* Knife and fork in steel with composition handles; $5–7 each. *Right:* Graniteware teapot; $26–32. All 1900–10. Both durable and attractive (it came in a variety of mottled colors ranging from gray to blue and green), graniteware was a great favorite with prairie settlers. ▼

Graniteware cooking pot; 1910–20; $20–30. This pot is gray, the most common graniteware color. In red, yellow, or brown it would command a substantially higher price. ▲

Cooking utensils in cast iron; 1895–1915. *Left:* Waffle iron, used at Gold Hill, Colo.; $30–35. *Center:* Meat grinder; by Interprise Manufacturing Co.; $25–35. *Right:* Frying pan; $12–17. Heavy but sturdy, cast iron was well suited to the rugged frontier life. ▶

Food chopper in tin and cast iron; 1895–1905; $70–85. Contraptions like this were the forerunners of modern food grinders and blenders. Most examples found in the West were made in eastern factories. ◀

Egg or produce basket in wire; 1900–20; ▲ $25–35. Though baskets made from natural fibers were widely used in the West, manufactured containers such as this were preferred for their durability.

Yellowware pottery; 1870–1900. *Left:* Blue sponge-decorated mixing bowl; ▲ $90–115. *Center:* Custard cup; $11–16. *Right:* Rolling pin; $55–65. Common yellowware from factories in New Jersey and Ohio was shipped west in large quantities. Mixing bowls appear to have been the most widely manufactured item.

Churn in wood with tin banding; 1870–80; $70–85. This factory-made churn is typical of many used on western farms. Milk products were an important part of the rural economy, and churning was traditional "woman's work." ▼

Butter-working tools; 1900–10; $8–12 each. *Left* and *Right:* Paddles used in working liquid out of newly made butter. *Center:* Ridged "Scotch Hand," one of a pair used to roll butter into small balls for table use. ▼

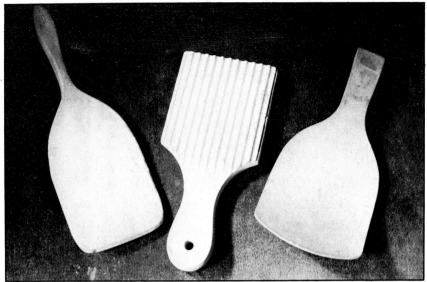

Butter molds; 1880–1900; $35–45 each. While some butter molds were hand carved, most were made at large factories like that of L.H. Mace in New York City and were transported to the plains by rail. ◄

Clock reel in ► western pine and maple; 1865–75; $75–100. Clock reels were used to measure yarn.

Portable patent knitting machine in ▲ cast iron; 1900–10; $45–55. Machines like these gradually replaced earlier wooden clothmaking equipment.

Flax spinning wheel in pine and ash; northern plains; 1865–75; $125–165. This wheel is European in style and may well have been brought west by or made by Scandinavian immigrants.
◀

Hooked seat cover; 1900–15; $45–55. Seat covers softened ▶ the rough splint or rawhide seating found in frontier homes.

Whirligig in painted pine; 1930–40; $250–300. Whirligigs, or▲ wind toys, have long been a popular decoration for sheds and porch rails. They were made throughout the country in large quantities during the 1930–50 period.

Front: Child's armchair in pine and hardwood; 1870–80; $75–90. *Rear:* Factory-made sidechair in pine and maple; 1890–1910; $45–55. These two pieces reflect the difference between local craftsmanship and factory-made furniture.
◀

225

8.

Where Roads and Rivers Met

The great cities of the West did not spring into being overnight. Like the metropolises of the Atlantic coast, they started out as small communities located at strategic crossroads or on favored harbors. Unlike their eastern counterparts, however, they did in many cases undergo periods of fabulous growth during which populations doubled or trebled and new sections *did* grow up almost overnight. This happened usually in response to a sudden economic change such as the establishment of a railroad or the discovery of nearby goldfields.

Before they were cities, these communities were towns—and often unattractive ones at that. The land was raw, building materials often were scarce, and the resulting urban conglomeration could be unsightly.

Such conditions could be attributed to the great influx of people occasioned by land grants and gold strikes. San Francisco was a sleepy Spanish town until the momentous events at Sutter's Mill. Then in a matter of days it became the terminus for hundreds of ships bearing men destined for the gold hills and merchandise for the shopkeepers who were supplying them. Under such crowded and chaotic conditions there was little time for the niceties of urban design. As the demand for living and working space increased, land prices skyrocketed.

Noise and violence were more or less characteristic of most towns. Populations were overwhelmingly male, and what women there were were likely to be bawdy house girls. Moreover, these men—miners, cowboys, mule skinners, tough loggers from the northern woods—were an unruly lot, drawn, in many cases, from the dregs of society. In the East, they would have been in jail. In the West, they were on the streets with a snoot full of whiskey and a gun in their belt.

These westerners worked hard and lived hard. Their lives were dangerous, and when they had money to spend and time to spend it, they wanted their sort of entertainment: gambling dens, saloons, and red-light districts. With the exception of those few communities that had been established by religious groups, every town west of the Mississippi provided these services in abundance.

Saloons and hotels were not the only business establishments. Any town worth its salt had a variety of business houses. Banking was extremely important because mining and land transactions required not only large sums of money but skilled financial employees as well. There were also assay offices, bullion houses, and jewelers, all trades associated with the mining industry.

Nothing was more important to the community than the general store. It was more than a place where one could purchase goods—in a very real sense it was the heart of the community.

The storekeeper was more than a merchant. He often knew more than anyone else about goings on in the community. If there was no hotel, the stage stopped at his door. He supplied grub and equipment for prospectors (more than one merchant got rich on a claim share exchanged for twenty-dollar's worth of groceries) and so had a pretty good idea of local mineral wealth. On Saturdays, he saw most of the farmers from surrounding areas, so he was up on agriculture and also in a good position to do some land and timber speculation.

Because most of the town gossip circulated around his stove in winter or hovered over his front porch in summer, he became the most likely if not the most accurate source of local news. He was, in short, merchant, banker, land agent, and newsman all rolled into one.

The closest thing to him was the town doctor. He probably didn't have a medical degree, most didn't back then, and most of the great killers like cholera and smallpox were beyond his resources. But he could remove bullets, set bones, deliver babies, and he was a part of the community. Seldom rich or even well to do, he took a chicken or a cord of wood for his services without a second thought.

These were the basics. As the towns grew and prospered, they were joined by a multitude of others: professionals, such as lawyers and dentists; artisans, from tinsmiths to carpenters; merchants of everything imaginable. And as the towns and cities changed, so did the lives of their inhabitants. Families that had arrived in the West only a few years previously with a couple of chairs and a trunk or two prospered and grew. They built fine houses and found themselves able to afford the best items that local manufacturers could produce or even the better-grade factory-made products made in the East.

Preceding pages: *Left:* Water barrel in oak with iron banding; $35–45. *Center:* Hitching post in cast iron; $75–90. *Right:* Rustic armchair; $80–95. All 1890–1910.

Trade and Business Collectibles

The western trade and business community has spawned a host of collectible objects that range from office furnishings to advertising art. Although closely related to similar objects found in other areas of the country, these often have a particular western quality.

Some of the earliest and most interesting items are those related to the various small businesses and crafts upon which the prairie towns were dependent. These include the tools and equipment used by the artisan or shopkeeper as well as those things that he used to promote his business.

Bold, graphic shop signs and three-dimensional figures, such as those commonly found outside cigar stores, reflect a period when literacy was limited, streets crowded, and the need for instant recognition paramount. In days when it was not unusual for major hotels to announce the dinner hour by a trumpet blast or drum roll, it was hardly surprising that a tobacco-products seller would wheel a six-foot cigar-smoking Pocahontas out on his sidewalk or a shoe repairman would announce his presence by dangling a giant boot above his door.

In such a turbulent place and time, advertising items of this nature ran a certain risk. Overhead signs were a favorite target for local marksmen.

Such tragedies notwithstanding, quite a few of these unique items have survived. Understandably, in light of the western preoccupation with the red man, many feature Indians, particularly the posters used by druggists to advertise the alcohol-laden patent medicines that they recommended without hesitation for everything from the common cold to leprosy.

Though craft-related collectibles are relatively abundant, the greatest source of collectibles is the general store. Since the town storekeeper had to stock just about everything from shoes to farm equipment, his emporium was a veritable period museum. Among the more popular items associated with the general store are the large cast-iron coffee grinders and the many different tins for spices and foodstuffs.

Another interesting and considerably less exploited area is that of the furniture and equipment used in early business offices. There were desks, files, and, of course, typewriters. The prototype for the contemporary typewriter was first successfully marketed in 1878, by the Remington Company. However, between 1875 and 1925 a large number of competing models, many of them quite novel, were manufactured.

◀ Tobacconist's figure in polychromed wood; 1880–95; $4,500–5,000. Although not of the best quality, this cigar-store Indian brings a high price, reflecting the tremendous amount of current interest in folk sculpture.

Mill weight in cast iron; 1875–85; $400–475. Both folky and rare, mill weights command a high price when they appear on the market. This one is in the form of a horse, but they appear also as sheep, cows, and chickens. ▼

Shoe repairman's sign in ▶ wood; Boulder, Colo.; 1910–20; $300–375. The use of symbols representing a trade or business dates to medieval times and has always been more prevalent in cultures with a high rate of illiteracy. As more Americans learned to read, shop symbols vanished from most stores.

Painted woodenware;
1870–1900. *Left:* Trencher, or
chopping bowl; $100–125.
Center top: Spice box; $25–35.
Center bottom: Covered sugar
bucket; $55–70. *Right:*
Cheesebox; $40–50. Original
paint enhances the value of all
antiques.

Left: Grain scoop in wood; ▶
$13–18. *Center bottom:* Grain
scoop in tin; $7–10. *Right:* Set of
grain measures; $85–110 the set.
All 1890–1910.

230

▲

Top: Hay hooks; $8–24 each. *Center left:* Food chopper;
$30–40. *Center right:* Grain sifter; $25–30. *Bottom left:*
Wood clamp; $12–16. *Bottom center:* Large hay knife;
$70–85. *Bottom right:* Barrel plane; $40–50.

Left: Pair of brass-tipped horse hames; $17–26. *Right:* Single ▶
tree; $10–15. The horse and wagon were essential to
western travel, and horse and wagon tack is among the
most available and reasonably priced of western
memorabilia.

Butcher's sign in cast iron; Denver, Colo.; 1910–30; $225–275. Factory-made signs such as this are of less interest to collectors than homemade one-of-a-kind examples.

▼

Tailor's equipment. *Left:* Charcoal-burning iron in cast iron; 1870–80; $45–60. *Right:* Pair of shears in wrought steel; 1880–90; $25–35. In the days before the development of large clothing factories, the local tailor played a major role in dressing the community.

◄ Occupational shaving mugs; 1900–15. *Left:* $75–90. *Center:* $45–60. *Right:* $25–35. In a period when the barber shop functioned as a type of social club, it was customary for regular customers to have their own, personalized mug.

▲
Typewriter in black and gold; by L.C. Smith & Bros.; 1900–20; $55–70. This standard keyboard machine, by a major manufacturer, is still in good working order.

▲
Advertising poster in lithographed cardboard for Chief Two Moon Bitter Oil; 1920–30; $125–165. Hailed as a "wonderful laxative," Bitter Oil was just one of the many patent or nonprescription medicines found in the typical drugstores.

Home Furnishings

Where the farm household was usually content with enameled tin and ironstone for its table, the shopkeeper might prefer the new electroplated silver that was being shipped west in quantity from the great factories in Connecticut. He might complement this with Ohio graniteware, but he would be more likely to order French Haviland china or some white earthenware from Leeds in England. Despite the "buy American" campaigns waged by local manufacturers and labor groups, it was not until the very late nineteenth century that well-to-do American consumers could be weaned away from European china and pottery.

Furniture was another matter. It was exclusively domestic, but rarely western in origin. The freights from the East brought in vast quantities of richly carved rosewood and mahogany in the latest Victorian styles, and for those with tighter budgets, there was oak or pine from Grand Rapids, painted and grained to resemble the more exotic timbers.

While changes were taking place throughout the home, in most areas they were primarily changes of style, not of substance. In the kitchen and other work areas, however, a real transformation was being wrought. Carpet sweepers were appearing, and after them came the first vacuum cleaners, replacing the broom and the laborious task of hand sweeping the rugs. The mechanical sewing machine, developed by

Isaac Singer in 1851, was rapidly supplanting hand stitching, and patent egg beaters, meat grinders, and food choppers were all serving to reduce the time spent in the kitchen.

Much of the newly won free time was spent on personal pleasure and family entertainment, activities generally unavailable to the farmer. The stereoscope, developed by mid-century, provided lifelike views of faraway places, and stereo viewing became a popular evening pastime. Even more popular was the "talking machine," or phonograph.

Children benefited, too. Unlike their rural counterparts, the children of well-to-do city families were not depended upon as extra workers, and childhood, once a fleeting thing, was extended. Toys were no longer made by hand as a labor of love (and economy), but were made in factories and were purchased at local stores or through mail-order catalogs.

All the above-mentioned items are now very collectible. Phonographs and stereoscopes have been the rage for some time now, and more enthusiasts than ever before are seeking out carpet sweepers, apple slicers, and other humble domestic contrivances. Victorian furniture is in great demand throughout the country. The toy craze is phenomenal; some cast-iron banks and pull toys are presently worth more than a new automobile.

Castor set in electroplated silver with pressed-glass accessories; 1875–85; $65–90. Displayed as a centerpiece and useful for holding such things as salt and vinegar, the castor set personified the Victorian blending of luxury and practicality. ▼

▲
Tea set in electroplated silver; made in Connecticut and used in Colorado; 1890–1900; $135–200. Electroplate offers one of the best buys on the current antiques market.

Rear view of pony cart; 1890–1910; $900–1,100. This
attractive cart was used in Colorado. Note the wicker seats,
which swing out for easier access. ▼

Child's dogcart; 1915–25; $185–245. Though used for ▲
transportation by the Plains Indians, dogs never served this
role with settlers. The late-Victorian dogcart was a toy and a
curiosity rather than a practical conveyance.

Firefighter's ladder-and-hose carrier in cast iron, steel, and ▶
wood; by Caswell Co., Chicago Ill.; 1880; $5,000–7,500.
Used in Idaho Springs, Colo.

Neoclassic-style coffeepot in electroplated silver; by Pairpoint Manufacturing Co.; 1890–95; $85–115. Electroplating was a relatively simple manufacturing process that used a limited amount of silver per piece, making it possible to sell "silver" at a price within the reach of many city dwellers. ▼

Flatwear in electroplated silver; by Rogers Brothers; ▲ 1900–15; $2–4 apiece. Rogers silver was made in great quantity. *Center:* Portrait plate in hand-painted porcelain; 1910–20; $75–95.

◄ Pitcher in white earthenware; Ohio; 1900–10; $35–45. This piece is typical of the whiteware shipped west for kitchen and everyday use.

▲
Cookie jar in hand-painted porcelain with electroplated silver fittings; made in Germany; 1880–90; $80–110.

Cream and sugar set in pressed ► glass; 1870–80; $45–65. Mass-produced pattern glass was the poor man's cut crystal, and it was manufactured in hundreds of different patterns, all of which are collectible.

236

◄ Crystal chandelier; 1910–20; $475–575. Many of the major hotels and ballrooms as well as some private homes in the larger western cities were lighted by chandeliers, usually imported from abroad. This example is relatively late.

◄ Kerosene table lamp in pressed glass and brass with green shade; 1880–1900; $80–110. The availability of kerosene in the West led to the proliferation of fancy kerosene lamps like this. Initially they were owned only by the well-to-do, but, with decreasing fuel prices, they were made available to all.

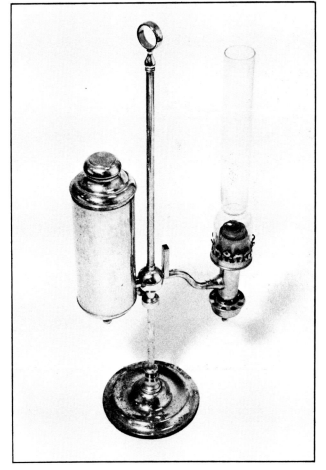

Student lamp in brass; 1870–85; $220–280. Student lamps ► are a great favorite with collectors. This one should be equipped with an appropriate shade.

◄ Garden fountain in cast iron; western Colorado; 1880–1900; $1,600–2,200. A lavish fountain was often the mark of the prosperous western businessman or mine owner; in an area where water was scarce, the ability to waste it was a sign of true affluence.

Detail of painted rams' heads in cast iron on garden fountain; western Colorado; 1880–1900; $1,600–2,200. The use of this decorative motif may have been inspired by the presence of mountain goats in the nearby hills. ▼

◄
Gazebo in wood and shingle; Georgetown, Colo. During the late 19th century, gazebos were constructed both in public parks and on private property. They served as bandstands, teahouses, and simply as a place to sit and admire the magnificent Rocky Mountain sunsets.

Overstuffed ▶
Victorian
Renaissance
Revival-style side-
chair; 1880–1900;
$90–125. Made
in sets of as many
as a dozen, these
popular pieces of
seating furniture
were found in
both living and
dining rooms.

Child's rocker in wicker; 1890–1900; $135–175. The ▶
elaborate design indicates that this is an early piece. Current
popularity has pushed wicker furniture prices to an all-time
high.

Early automatic ▶
vacuum cleaner; the
National; patented
in 1911; $75–90.
Attractively
decorated in gold on
a green ground, the
National was one of
the forerunners of
the contemporary
vacuum cleaner.

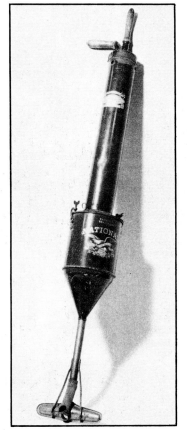

Electric sewing machine; the E-Z Sew, by Hamilton Beach; ▲
patented 1886; $90–130. One of the earliest electric sewing
machines, the Hamilton Beach is sought by collectors
entering this new field.

Phonograph; Edison Home ▶
Phonograph; patented 1898;
$375–450. Phonographs
changed the recreational life of
the nation, particularly in isolated
areas where professional
entertainment was rare. They are
a hot area for contemporary
collectors.

Toy stove in cast iron complete with
miniature pots and pans; Colorado;
1890–1900; $110–130. Developments in the
kitchen were often mirrored in children's toys.▼

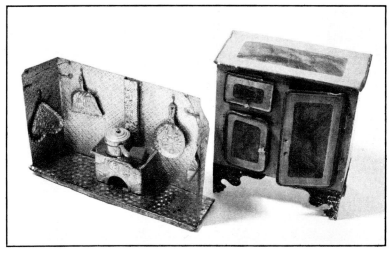

Tin toys; 1890–1910. *Left:* Stamped tin miniature kitchen; ▲
$65–80. *Right:* Brown-grained icebox; $45–60. Stamped
from sheet tin and assembled by hand, toys like these could
be made and sold inexpensively.

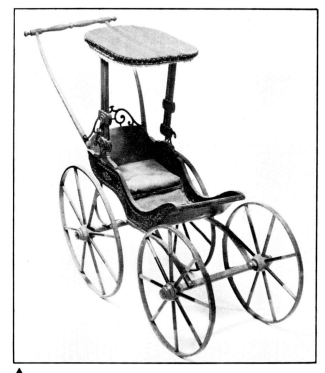

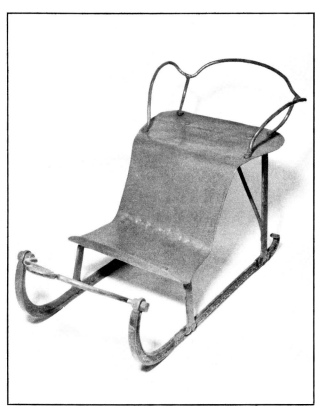

▲
Child's doll carriage in the Victorian manner in cast iron and
wood; 1880–1900; $175–200. Original paint and fringed
cloth top make this a highly desirable example of an
uncommon toy.

◄

Child's sled in sheet steel and cast iron; 1900–15; $95–115.
Children's sleds and sleighs tended to be miniature replicas
of those used by their parents. Some were even rigged to
be pulled by ponies or dogs.

Early western bottles; 1870–1880. *Left:* ▲ Warner's Safe Kidney Cure, a popular alcohol-base tonic; $15–22. *Center:* Historical flask marked "For Pike's Peak"; $75–90. This is a particularly important piece and bears the embossed portrait of a prospector who symbolizes the many who sought gold in the hills around Colorado's highest mountain. *Right:* Common green-glass whiskey bottle; $8–12.

Counter-size cigar-store Indian in ▶ polychromed wood and plaster; 1900–15; $1,500–2,000. The Indian as the tobacconists' trade mark appeared late in the West, no doubt because real Indians remained a threat until late in the 19th century.

Roulette wheel and table; 1885–95; $2,600–3,200. This ▶ wheel was used in a gambling casino in Broadmoor, Colo. Gambling was a major pastime (often with disastrous results) of both cowboys and miners.

9.

The Eskimos

Eskimo Art

The artistic tradition of the North American Eskimo is very old, and art objects made in the fifth century B.C. are frequently found in advanced collections. These pieces have more going for them than mere age: the powerful combination of naturalism and abstraction achieved by Inuit artists has made their work among the most sought after of all folk crafts.

When we speak of Eskimo art, the reference is primarily to sculpture. There is painting, from masks to cave art, and some contemporary lithography, but sculpted objects predominate.

Moreover, all such art is religious in nature, reflecting an attempt by the artist to use his skills to control his environment. The Inuit were animists, believing that all things, including those that they made, had a soul. These souls or spirits had mobility and the power to affect the lives of men. Because they lived primarily by

hunting, the tribes were concerned with the spirits of the animals they slew, for, if not appeased, these might work vengeance by spoiling the hunt or, worse, causing an accident.

To ward off such occurrences, Eskimo artists have for generations carved effigy figures of the seal, walrus, whale, caribou, and other animals that they hunted. Such sculptures are small, usually less than three inches long or tall, and are rendered in a highly formal and stylized manner that minimizes all but the most essential characteristics. Such art was put to varied uses: some pieces were tied to weapons and hunting clothing to bring luck in the chase; some were used by the tribal shamans, or *angekoks,* in ceremonies intended to achieve the same result; while yet others were gambling tokens used in traditional games.

Whatever their intended purpose, the tiny figures

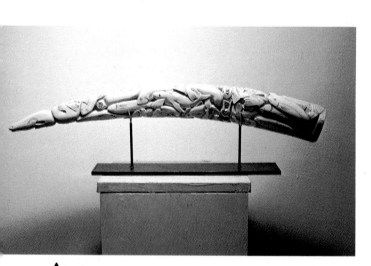

▲
Elaborately carved walrus tusk; Nunivak Island; 1915–25; $3,300–3,700. The sort of detail evidenced in this trade piece would take many days to achieve and reflects the hand of a master carver.

Torso in ivory; Old Bering Sea Culture; 350 B.C.–A.D. 300; ▶ $6,500–7,000. Prehistoric Eskimo art is neither well known nor widely collected, and most major pieces are owned by museums or a few sophisticated collectors.

Preceding pages: Bear carved in old ivory; St. Lawrence Island, Alaska; 1100–1300; $1,500–1,750. Eskimo carving was done in fossilized ivory found buried in the permafrost, in old ivory gathered along beaches, or in walrus ivory taken in the hunt.

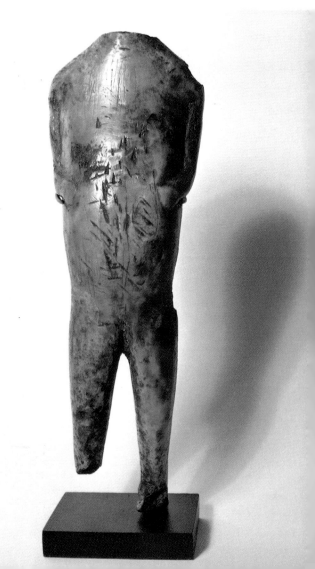

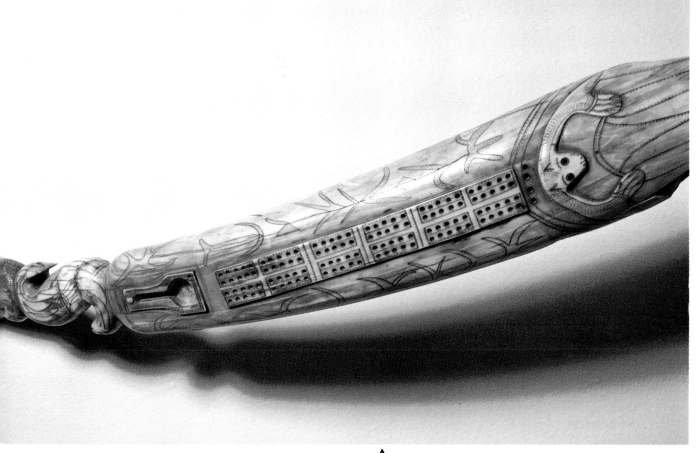

▲
Detail of cribbage board in carved ivory; Nunivak Island; 1890–1900; $3,500–4,000. Eskimo carvers employ three types of ivory, all derived from walrus tusk: new ivory, which is white; old ivory that has turned tan from exposure to the elements (such as this piece); and dark-brown fossil ivory.

were sculpted with great care, usually from ivory, which was available in quantity either in its fresh white state from newly slain walruses or whales or as "old" ivory found on beaches or at the last resting places of the great mastodons that once roamed the area.

Wood was preferred for larger work, particularly among the forest-dwelling Inuit of the southern Alaskan coast. Their carving focused on the masks employed by the shamans in elaborate rituals intended to control the evil spirits with which Eskimo mythology abounded. These spirits, if left to their own devices, could cause illness and natural disaster, but once forced to enter the masks, they could be subjugated or appeased.

As the old magic waned, these masks took on a new function: amusement. At intertribal meetings dancers would vie to see who could provoke the most laughter with his mask and his antics. Thus the falsefaces, which were often composed of bizarre and seemingly unrelated elements, existed in a strange world between fear and laughter, and even today few Inuit treat them lightly.

Since Eskimo sculpture is so closely related to

▲
Doll's head in carved wood; Diomede Island; mid-19th century; $10,000–10,500. This outstanding example of Eskimo sculptural art was found in Alaska and is a one-of-a-kind piece. Its simplicity and strong graphic quality are typical of the best early Eskimo carving.

247

Miniature head carved in fossilized ivory; Okvik Culture; 500–100 B.C.; $2,500–3,000. As animists, the Eskimos saw everything around them, including their carvings, as endowed with a spirit or life. Masks of this sort were often used in rituals by shamans, or medicine men.

Miniature geese carved in ivory; Thule culture; 1100–1300; ▶ $50–75 each. These carvings are gambling pieces used in a game called ting miu jang. The two players sit opposite each other and, in turn, throw a group of counters into the air. Any that fall upright facing the thrower become his.

Miniature ducks ▶ carved in old ivory; Fort Barrow, Alaska; 1930–40; $175–200. Though carved as toys or for the tourist trade, these finely worked pieces reflect an ongoing sculptural tradition that can be traced back to the Thule period.

Hunting amulet in ▶ the form of a face carved in wood; Brevig Mission, Alaska; late 18th century; $850–950. While wood was readily available to the forest Eskimos, those tribes residing on the coast had to use driftwood.

◀ Walrus-head amulet carved in ivory; 500–1000; $1,250–1,500. Much of Eskimo art was directed at placating the spirits of dead animals so that they would not warn away the living ones that the hunter sought. Hunters wore lucky amulets on their hats and clothing.

248

hunting and to survival in a difficult environment, one might assume that as their creators' life-styles changed with the advance of white culture the carvings would gradually vanish. That has not happened. During the nineteenth century, Inuit artwork found a market among white traders and explorers, and since 1945, worldwide appreciation has led to increased demand for sculpture. There have been changes, however.

Faced with a shortage of the traditional ivory, the carvers have substituted soapstone and jade. As hunting ceases to be a way of life, the traditional hunting subjects are being replaced with domestic scenes. Exposed to other artistic influences, the artists modify their styles. Yet the basic creative drive remains, and after over 2,500 years, Eskimo art remains alive and well in the frozen North.

Hunting and Household Implements

Given the extremely difficult conditions under which they lived and the limited raw materials available to them, the variety of household and hunting accessories produced by the Inuit is truly amazing. Most of these implements, in both the prehistoric and historic periods, were made from bone, walrus or fossil-mastadon ivory or whalebone, or narwhale tusk when available. Stone was used as well, and wood when it could be obtained. Wood appears in many items manufactured by the Eskimos living along the forested coast of southwestern Alaska, but it is used with less frequency by the northern coastal tribes. It was so precious in the treeless northern tundra that small pieces of driftwood were sometimes pegged or bound together to make larger things, such as hunting hats and boat frames.

As with their sculpture, the tools made by Eskimos are characterized by extreme simplicity of form and a high degree of care. Until metal-cutting tools became available, during the nineteenth century, carving and cutting were done with stone or bone implements. Even so, remarkable effects were achieved.

Because the Inuit believed that the objects they made became imbued with a spirit life of their own and could bring good or ill luck, the carver's skill was very much in his or her interest. In no other area was this more important than that of hunting implements. The Eskimos were almost completely dependent on wild game for their survival, and they produced many different weapons and tools for use in the hunt. There were wooden harpoons, spear throwers, and bows. As these were of prime importance to the huntsman, they were frequently carved with elaborate talismanic designs

intended to placate animal spirits that might bring storms or spoil the hunt.

Shaped with less elaboration, perhaps, but of almost equal importance, were knives, fishhooks and hook straighteners, sinkers, arrowheads and arrow sharpeners, and the wooden plugs used to fill wounds in the bodies of slain animals so that the blood could be preserved for food.

Another group of tools was necessary to process meat and skins. These included bone or stone scrapers for cleaning hides; a variety of fletching, or dressing, knives; hooks on which to hang the catch; and the "woman's" knife, or *ulo*, an all-purpose tool used in many cooking and household tasks.

Much more elaborate decoration is found on smoking utensils, especially pipes and tobacco boxes. These were prized possessions, and were usually embellished with scrimshaw work, the incising of fine lines in the surface that were then filled in with lampblack or vegetable coloring. Scrimshaw pipes, cribbage boards, and small boxes were among the first Eskimo artifacts to attract the white man's eye.

Clothing was made of leather, but so were many other useful things, such as bait bags, water buckets, dogsled harnesses, fishnets and fish line, and even the stone- or bone-weighted cords, known as bolas, that were used to bring down small birds.

With the gradual integration of the Inuit into white society and the increasing availability of modern weapons, tools, and clothing, the need for handmade implements has all but vanished. The remaining examples can only continue to increase in value.

Toy kayak; Canadian Eskimo; late 19th century; $1,200–1,400. This piece is made of walrus skin stretched on a wooden frame and sewn together with gut—the same method used to construct full-size boats. ▼

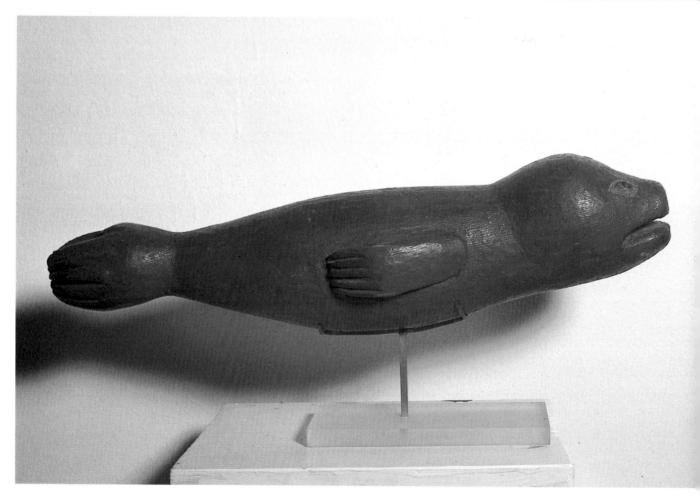

Ceremonial shaman's club; western Alaska; mid-19th ▲ century; $4,500–5,000. The red-painted seal reflects the Eskimo preoccupation with an important source of food and raw materials.

Shaman's, or wizard's, hat in wood and feathers painted red and black; Nunivak Island; 1920–25; $4,000–4,500. The basic decorative motif is a seal with a superimposed face possibly intended to represent the sun.

Fragment of ceremonial drum; Kuskokwim River, Alaska; ▲ 1870–80; $12,500–13,000. The rim is of wood and the handle is of ivory carved in the form of a walrus. A very rare piece.

◄

Death mask; Hooper Bay, Alaska; 1875–95; $3,500–4,000. The white paint and feathers create a striking and almost frightening aspect—no doubt just what the carver hoped to achieve.

Arrow straightener in prehistoric mastodon ivory; 19th
century; $110–120. This tool was in constant use among a
people who depended on the spear and bow for most of
their food. ▼

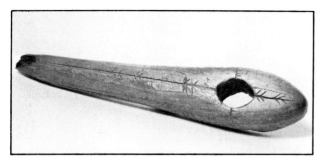

Wound plug in wood carved in the likeness of a walrus; ▲
1850–70; $850–900. Blood was an important source of
nourishment to the Inuit, and plugs such as this were used to
stop bleeding in animals slain in the hunt.

Comb in ivory; ▶
Alaska; late 18th
century; $100–110.
Combs such as this
were used for
combing not only
human hair but that
on hides as well.

Woman's ▶
knife, or *ulo*, in
ivory and
steel; Nunivak;
1920–30;
$450–500. The
handle of this
knife is carved
in the shape of
a fox.

◀ Pair of sun goggles in whalebone;
1870–90; $250–300. The reflection
of sun on snow raised the threat of
snow blindness, so Eskimos used
goggles like these and large
wide-brimmed hats.

Pair of harpoon shafts in ivory;
mid-19th century; $100–125 each.
In a land where wood was scarce,
bone was used for bows and spear
shafts. ▼

◀ Ladle in wood; Shishmaref, Alaska; late 18th
century; $120–135. Destruction by the elements
has made early wooden tools relatively
uncommon.

Acknowledgments

Caboose Antiques, Nederland, Colorado
Taylor Museum—Colorado Springs Fine Arts Center, Colorado Springs, Colorado
Colorado Railroad Museum, Golden, Colorado
Buffalo Bill Museum, Golden, Colorado
Historic Mining and Milling Museum, Idaho Springs, Colorado
Pioneer Museum, Boulder, Colorado
Myers & Ellman, New York, New York
Barbara Rohrs, New York, New York
Central Gold Mine, Mining and Historical Museum, Central City, Colorado
Dorthy Morin, Denver, Colorado
Joe Dusek, Denver, Colorado

Jim Wardell, Denver, Colorado
Two Sisters Antiques and Collectibles, Denver, Colorado
Ellen's Antiques, Denver, Colorado
University of Colorado Museum, Boulder, Colorado
Pioneers' Museum, Colorado Springs, Colorado
Pro Rodeo Hall of Champions, Colorado Springs, Colorado
Western Museum of Mining & Industry, Colorado Springs, Colorado
El Pomar Carriage Museum, Broadmoor, Colorado
Smith Gallery, New York, New York
Alan S. Kelley, Middlebury, Connecticut
Steve Miller, New York, New York
Maxwell Museum of Anthropology, Albuquerque, New Mexico
Museum of International Folk Art, Santa Fe, New Mexico
The American Cowboy Gallery, Colorado Springs, Colorado

Bibliography

The Original Americans
Bunzel, Ruth J. *The Pueblo Potter: A Study of Creative Imagination in Primitive Art.* New York: Dover, 1972.
Douglas, Frederick, and D'Harnoncourt, Rene. *Indian Art of the United States.* New York: Arno Press, 1969.
Hothem, Lar. *North American Indian Artifacts.* Florence, Ala.: Books Americana, 1978.
James, George W. *Indian Blankets and Their Makers.* New York: Dover, 1974.
Mauer, Evan M. *The Native American Heritage: A Survey of North American Indian Art.* Lincoln, Nebr.: University of Nebraska Press, 1977.
Tanner, Clara Lee. *Prehistoric Southwest Craft Arts.* Tucson, Ariz.: University of Arizona Press, 1976.
Vidler, Virginia. *American Indian Antiques.* New York: A. S. Barnes & Co., 1975.
Whitford, Andrew H. *North American Indian Arts.* New York: Golden Press, 1970.

The Spanish Colonists
Andrews, Ruth, ed. *How to Know American Folk Art.* New York: Dutton, 1977.
Comstock, Helen, ed. *The Concise Encyclopedia of American Antiques.* New York: Hawthorne Books.
Dobie, J. Frank. *Coronado's Children.* Dallas: Southwest Press, 1930.
Duffus, R. L. *The Santa Fe Trail.* New York: Longmans, Green & Co., 1930.
Hafen, LeRoy, R. *Old Spanish Trail.* Glendale, Calif.: Arthur H. Clark Co., 1954.
Hammond, George P., and Rey, Agapito. *Don Juan de Onate, Colonizer of New Mexico, 1595–1628.* Albuquerque, N.Mex.: University of New Mexico Press, 1953.
Wilder, Mitchell A., and Breitenbach, Edgar. *Santos—The Religious Folk Art of New Mexico.* Colorado Springs, Colo.: privately published, 1943.

Mountain Men and Buffalo Runners
Beitz, Les. *Treasury of Frontier Relics.* South Brunswick, N.J. and New York: A. S. Barnes & Co., 1977.
Boatright, Mody C. *Folk Laughter on the Frontier.* New York: Macmillan Co., 1949.
Chittenden, Hiram M. *The American Fur Trade of the Far West* (3 vols.). New York: F. P. Harper, 1902, 1935.
Cleland, Robert G. *This Reckless Breed of Men.* New York: Alfred A. Knopf, 1950.
Davidson, Leverette J., and Blake, Forrester, eds. *Rocky Mountain Tales.* Norman, Okla.: University of Oklahoma Press, 1947.
Monaghan, Jay, ed. *The Book of the American West.* New York: Bonanza Books, 1963.

Days of Forty-nine
Beitz, Les. *A Treasury of Frontier Relics.* South Brunswick, N. J., and New York: A. S. Barnes & Co., 1977
Hulburt, Arthur B. *Forty Niners: The Chronicle of the California Trail.* Boston: Little, Brown & Co., 1949.
Jenkins, Olaf P., ed. *The Mother Lode Company.* San Francisco: State of California, Division of Mines, 1948.
Karsner, David. *Silver Dollar.* New York: Covici–Friede, 1932.
Lewis, Oscar. *Silver Kings.* New York: Alfred A. Knopf, 1947.
Smith, Grant H. *History of the Comstock Lode.* Reno, Nev.: Nevada State Bureau of Mines, 1943.

The Iron Road
Hollingsworth, J. B., and Whitehouse, P. B. *North American Railways.* Hong Kong: Bison Books, 1977.
Klamkin, Charles. *Railroadiana.* New York: Funk & Wagnalls, 1976.
McPherson, James A., and Williams, Miller. *Railroad Trains and Train People in American Culture.* New York: Random House, 1976.
Riegel, Robert E. *The Story of the Western Railroads.* New York: Macmillan Co., 1926.
Western Writers of America. *Trails of the Iron Horse.* Garden City, N.Y.: Doubleday & Co., Inc., 1975.

The Cowboys
Adams, Ramon F. *The Old Time Cowhand.* New York: Macmillan Co., 1961.
Botkin, B. A., ed. *A Treasury of Western Folklore.* New York: Crown, 1951.
Dole, Edward. *The Range Cattle Industry.* Norman, Okla.: University of Oklahoma Press, 1930.
Dobie, J. Frank. *The Longhorns.* Boston: Little, Brown & Co., 1941.
Woods, Jim, ed. *Guns of the Gunfighters.* Los Angeles: Peterson Publishing Co., 1975.

They Plowed the Plains
Beck, Doreen. *Collecting Country and Western Americana.* New York: Hamlyn, 1975.
Ghent, W. J. *The Road To Oregon: A Chronicle of the Great Emigrant Trail.* New York: Tudor Publishing Co., 1934.
Ketchum, William C. Jr. *The New and Revised Catalog of American Antiques.* New York: Rutledge-Mayflower, 1980.
Pound, Louise. *Nebraska Folklore.* Lincoln: University of Nebraska Press, 1959.
Winther, Oscar O. *The Old Oregon Country, A History of Frontier Trade, Transportation and Travel.* Stanford, Calif.: Stanford University Press, 1950.

Where Roads and Rivers Met
Bishop, Robert, and Coblentz, Patricia. *The World of Antiques, Art and Architecture in Victorian America.* New York: E. P. Dutton, 1979.
Botkin, B. A., ed. *A Treasury of Western Folklore.* New York: Crown, 1951.
Mackay, James. *Collectables.* London: Macdonald & Jones, 1979.

The Eskimos
Carpenter, Edmund. *Eskimo Realities.* New York: Holt, Rinehart & Winston, 1973.
Carson, I. A. Ritchie. *Bone and Horn Carving: A Pictorial History.* South Brunswick, N. J., and New York: A. S. Barnes and Co., 1975.
Carson, I. A. Ritchie. *Art of the Eskimo.* South Brunswick, N. J., and New York: A. S. Barnes & Co., 1979.

Index

Numbers in italics refer to illustrations.

Acoma Pueblo, pottery, 44, *45*
Advertising
    business, 229, *229, 232*
    railroad, 196, *198, 200–02, 206*
Anvils, *155*
Apache Indians, 10, 21, 60, 141
    baskets, 47, *48, 49*
Aragon, José Rafael, 68, *69*
Archuleta, Manuel, 61, *63*
Arikara Indians, 12
Ashley, William, 84
Axes, *91*

Badges, railroad, 188, *189*
Bannock Indians, *51*
Barbed wire, 96, 216, *218, 219*
Basketry, Indian, 12, 26, 47, *47–55, 48, 50*
Bass, Sam, 174
Beadwork, Indian, *18, 19, 23, 25, 27, 29, 30, 31, 93*
Beaver trapping, 84, 86, 88, 91
Bells, railroad, 181
Bits, horse, 105, *117*
Blackfoot Indians, 10, 12, 84, 86
Blankets and rugs, Indian, *19, 22, 32, 33, 35*
Blasting powder, 145, *150*
Bluecoats, 12, 13, 56, *56–57*
Boots, cowboy, 96, 105, *108, 109, 134, 135*
Bottles, *124*, 140, *242*
Bowie knives, 91, *91*, 140
Branding irons, 97, 105, *121*
Bridger, Jim, 86
Bridles, horse, 105, *117*
Buckets, farm, *212*
Buckets, ore, 144, 154, *158, 159, 212*
Buffalo, 10, 88, 91, 167
Buffalo hunters, 88, 91, 167
Bultos, 68, *69, 72, 75, 79*
Business equipment, 228–29, *229, 232*
Butter molds, 220, *224*
Buttons, railroad, 188, *189, 190*

Cabooses, 166, 170, *173*
Carpet sweepers, 233, *240*
Carretas, 60, 214
Cars, railway, 169–70, *171–73*, 204
Carson, Kit, 86
Cassidy, Butch, 168
Cattle, drives, 97–98, *103*, 166
Cattle, longhorn, 96–98, 166
Chaps, 105, *107*, 108
Cheyenne Indians, 166
Chiefs' blankets, 32
Chimayo Valley textiles, 76, *77, 80*
Chisholm, Jesse, 97
Chisholm Trail, 97, 167
Cigar-store Indians, 229, *229, 242*

Clock reels, *224*
Cochita Pueblo, baskets, 42
Cody, Buffalo Bill, 88, 91, 132
Coffee grinders, 229
Colcha stitch, 76, *81*
Colt handguns, 132, *133*
Colt, Samuel, 132
Colter, John, 84
Comanche Indians, 12, 97
Concord coaches, 214, *215*
Conestoga wagons, 212, 213, 214, *214, 215,* 220
Cooper, Peter, 169
Coronado, Francisco, 60
Coureurs de bois, 84
Cowboys
    amusements, 122, *242*
    clothing and equipment, 96, 105, *106–17, 119, 120, 130, 134, 135*
    musical instruments, 122, *125–28*
    weapons, *4*, 132, *133, 136–37*
Crow Indians, 12
Crowbars, 145, *149*
Crushers, ore, 154, *159*
Cuspidors, 196, *202*
Custer, Gen. George A., 12, 132

Da, Tony, 40
Derringers, 137
Digger Indians, 10
Dining car
    china, 204, *205*, 206
    glass, *203*, 204
    silverware, *203*
Dogcarts, 234
Drills, 144, 145, *149*
Dry farming, 213

Elevators, mining, 144, *146*, 154, *158, 159*
Eskimos, 246–47, *246*, 249
    carving, *245, 246,* 246–47, *247, 248, 250, 251*
    household and hunting items, 249, *252*
    masks, *251*
    scrimshaw, 249
    toys, *250*

Fareboxes, railway, 196
Farm implements
    barbed wire, 96, 216, *218, 219*
    bowls, wooden, *212*, 220, *221*
    butter molds, 220, *224*
    canning jars, 220
    churns, 220, *224*
    cookie cutters, 220, *222*
    grain measures, *230*

hay knives, 216, *217, 231*
hoes, 216
huskers, corn, 216
ox yokes, *210*, 216
pitch forks, 216
planters, corn and potato, 216, *217*
plows, 213, 216, *217*
potato mashers, *212*
rakes, 216
saws, *218*
scoops, *230*
scythes, 216
shovels, 216, *218*
sifters, *230*
spinning wheels, *225*
washing machines, 220
Fink, Mike, 86, 88
Fire engines, 234
Furniture, 61–62, *62, 63, 71, 79, 92*, 220, *225, 228, 229, 233, 240*
Fur traders, 12, 84, 86, 88, 91

Galloping Geese, 168, *172*
Gamblers, 122, *123, 242*
Garces, Francisco, 60
General store, 228, 229
Glass, 203, *203, 236*
Glass, Hugh, 86
Glidden, Joseph, 216
Gold, 140–41, 154, 166
Goodnight-Loving Trail, 97
Graniteware, 222
Greeley, Horace, 140
Green River knives, 91
Guns, 12, 56, *57, 88, 91*, 132, *133, 136–37*

Handcars, *195*
Harness, horse and burro, *155*
Hats, 93, 105, *106, 135*, 188, *189*
Hay knives, 216, *217, 231*
Headlights, railroad, 182, *183*
Helmets, mining, 144, *153*
Henry rifle, 88, 91, *89*
Hickok, Wild Bill, 132
Hidatsa Indians, *28*
Hopi Indians, 10, *11, 14,* 32, 38, *38, 39, 43, 46,* 50
Horn furniture, *92*
Horseshoes, *120*
Hudson Bay blankets, 32

Indians, 10, 12–13
    basketry, 26, 47, *47–55*
    battles and wars, 13
    beadwork, *18, 19, 23, 25, 27, 29, 30, 31*
    blankets and rugs, *19, 22, 32, 32–37*, 76
    clothing, 16, *18, 19, 23, 29*

crafts, *11*, *14*, 16, *23*, *25*, *29*, *32*
    dolls, *22*
    musical instruments, *25*, *28*
    paintings, *15*, *22*, *26*, *27*, *31*
    pipes, *14*, *25*, *28*
    pottery, *14*, *27*, *40*, *40–46*
    sculpture, *17*, *18*, 20
    weapons, *21*, *24*, *25*
Insulators, telegraph, 206, *207*
Isleta Pueblo, pottery, *46*
Ivory, eskimo, *245*, *246*, 247, *247*, *248*

James Brothers, 168

Kachinas, *11*, *14*, 38, *38–39*
Kentucky rifles, 91
Kerosene lamps 151, *152–53*, 182, *183*,
    185–86, 196, 220, 237
Keys, railroad, 188, *190*
Kitchenware, 63, *130*, 212, 220, *221–24*, 230,
    233, *249*, 252
Klamath Indians, basketry, 52, *53*

Labor-saving devices, 233
Lamps
    mining, 151, *152*, *153*
    railway, 176, *177*, *181–84*
Lighting devices, 151, *152*, *153*, 176, *177*, *181*,
    184, 220, 237
Little Big Horn, 13
Locks, railroad, 188, *190*
Locomotive identification plates, *175*
Locomotives, 169, *170–71*, 180, 194
Lopez, Felix, *78*
Lopez, José Dolores, 60, *68*
Lost River Indians, basketry, *52*

Makah Indians, basketry, *52*
Mandan Indians, crafts, 23, *28*, *29*
Maricopa Pueblo, pottery, *45*
Martinez family, potters, 40, *40*, *41*
Masterson, Bat, 132
Metalwork, 61–62, *63*, 64, 220, *222–23*
Mill weights, 229
Mills, ore, 144, 154
Mining
    air pump, *157*
    amalgamating tables, 154
    assaying tools, 160, *160–62*
    copper, *141*
    deeds, 163
    equipment, 140, *140*, *143*, 144, 145, *146*,
        147, *149*, *150*, *154–55*, *157–59*
    gold, 140–41, 154, 160
    helmets, 151, *153*
    lighting devices, 151, *152–53*
    photographs, *148*
    silver, *141*, 154, 160
    stock certificates, 160, *163*
Mojave Indians, pottery, *44*
Mono Indians, baskets, *51*
Mortars and pestles, 160, *162*
Mountain men, 84, *85*, *86*, 88, 91, 93
Mucker, mining, *157*
Musical instruments, 28, 122, *125–28*

Narrow-gauge railways, 167–68, *180*, 182
Navajo Indians, 22, 32, *32–37*, 47
Northwest Coast Indians, 24, *26*, *51*, 52, *53*

Ore cars, *140*, 143, 146, 154, *154*, *157*
Oregon Trail, 12
Oxen, 216

Pack saddle, 156
Paiute Indians, baskets, *47*, *51*
Pans, mining, 145, *148*
Papago Indians, 10, 47, *49*
Paper, 160, *163*, 174
Pawnee Indians, 10, 12
Peacemaker, 132, *133*
Pembina buggies, 214
Pendleton blankets, 32
Penitente figures, 60, *70*
Phonographs, 233, *240*
Pickaxes, 145, *148*, 149
Pima Indians, basketry, 49, *53*, 55
Pipes, Indian, *14*, *25*, *28*
Pit River Indians, baskets, *51*, *52*
Plains Indians, 10, *14*, 16, *18*, *19*, *27*, 29, *30*, *31*,
    60, 166
Planters, corn and potato, 216, *217*
Plows, 213, 216, *217*
Pokes, miners', 145
Pony carts, *234*
Pottery, 12, *14*, *27*, 40, *40–46*, 220, 233, *236*
Powder horns, 89, *90*, 91
Prairie schooners, 212, *213*, 214, *214*, *215*,
    220
Presentation lanterns, railway, *186*
Prospector's tools, *140*, 144, 145, *148*
Pueblo Indians, 10, 38, 60
Pullman, George M., 169–70

Quinault Indians, basketry, *52*

Railroad
    advertising, 196, *198*, *200–02*
    badges, 188, *189*
    bells, *175*
    blueprints, *174*
    buttons, 188, *189–90*
    cabooses, 166, 170
    cars, 166, 169–70, *171*, *172–73*, 182, 203
    china, 203, *205*, 206
    clothing and equipment, 188, *189–95*,
        197–98, 202
    communications devices, 206, *207–08*, 209
    fare boxes, 196
    furniture, *173*, 197
    glass, 203, *203*
    light, 176, *177*, *181*, *184*, 196
    locks and keys, 188, *190*
    locomotives, 169, *170–71*, 175, 180, *182*,
        183
    logbooks, *174*
    signal flags, *180*
    signs, *187*, 196, *199*
    silverware, 203
    ticket offices, 196
    whistles, *175*
Reins, horse, 105, *117*
Remington, Frederic, 99
Remington firearms, 4, 132
Retablos, 68, 72, *73*, *74*, *75*, *78*
Retorts, mining, 160
Rocky Mountain canaries, 154
Rocky Mountain Rendezvous, 84, 86
Rodeo, 98, 105, *112–13*, *115*, *117*, *118–19*,
    122

Roundups, 97, *100*, *103*
Rugs, 32, *32–37*, 76, *77*, *80–81*
Russell, Charles M., 99

Sabanillas, *81*
Saddles, 65, 98, *102*, 105, *110–13*, *114*, 130,
    156
San Ildefonso Pueblo, pottery, *40*, *41–42*
San Juan Pueblo, pottery, *43*, 46
San Lorenzo Pueblo, pottery, *46*
Santa Clara Pueblo, pottery, *43*
Santeros, 68
Santos, 60, 68, 69, *72*, *74*, *75*, *78*, *79*
Scales, gold and silver, 144, 160
Scrimshaw, 247, *249*
Seed beads, 16
Serapes, *34*, 76
Sewing machines, 233, *240*
Sharps rifles, 84, 88, *88*, 91
Shaving mugs, *232*
Shoshoni Indians, 12
Shovels, 145, *148*, *149*, 216, *218*
Sidesaddles, *112*
Signal flags, railroad, *180*
Signs, *187*, 196, *199–200*, 229, *229*, 232
Silver, *141*, 154, 160, 203, 233, *233*, *236*
Singer, Isaac, 233
Sioux Indians, *11*, 12, *23*, *27*, 30
Slag cars, mining, 159
Smith & Wesson, handguns, 4, *136*, 137
Smith, Jedediah S., 84
Spanish-American
    colchas, 76, *81*
    colonists, 10, 60–61, 84, 140
    furniture, 61–62, *62*, 63, *71*
    leatherwork 62, 65
    metal wares, 61–62, *63*, 64
    painting and sculpture, 60, 61, 68, 69, *72*,
        73, *74*, *75*, *78*
    sabanillas, *81*
    santeros, 68
    santos, 60, 68, *74*, *78*, *79*
    textiles, 61, 76, *77*, 80
Spencer rifles, 132
Spikes, *155*, 188, *193*
Spinning wheels, *225*
Spittoons, 196, *202*
Spurs, 64, 105, *116*
Stage coaches, 214
Steam engines, 169, *170–71*, 180, 182, *183*,
    194
Stereoscopes, 233
Sticking tommies, 151, *152*
Stock certificates, 160, *163*
Student lamps, 237
Suitcases, *215*
Sundance Kid, 168
Sutter, John, 86, 140, 168

Tank towns, 196
Taos Pueblo, pottery, *46*
Telegraph, *187*, 208
Telephones, 159, 206, *208–09*
Textiles, 32, *32–37*, 76, *77*, *80–81*, *225*
Ticket offices, railroad, 196
TicNosPos rugs, *33*
Tinware, 220, *222–23*
Tlingit Indians, *26*
Tobacco, 122, *128*, *129*

Tomahawks, *25*
Tools, *232*
Toys, 22, 233, 241, 250
Trade guns, 12, *87*
Trade signs, 229, *229, 232*
Trappers, 84, 86, 88, 91, *92, 93*
Traps, game, *91, 92*
Trolleys, 169, *186*
Typewriters, 229, *232*

U.S. military items, 12, 13, 56, *56–57*

Ute Indians, basketry, *50*

Vaqueros, 96

Walapai Indians, basketry, *48*
Weapons, 4, *11, 21,* 24, *25,* 56, *57, 84, 87, 88, 89, 90,* 91, *91,* 98, *132, 133, 136–37,* 249, *252*
Western Trail, 97
Whirligigs, *225*

Whistles, train, *175*
Williams, Old Bill, 86, 88
Winchester rifles, 132, *136*

Yei rugs, *35*
Yellowware pottery, 220, *223*
Yokes, *210,* 216

Zia Indians, pottery, 27, *46*
Zuni Indians, 10, 14, 38, *38,* 60